STANLEY MILGRAM
OBEDIENCE TO AUTHORITY
AN EXPERIMENTAL VIEW

STANLEY MILGRAM

Stanley Milgram was born in New York in 1933. A graduate of Queens College and Harvard University, he taught social psychology at Yale and Harvard Universities before becoming a Distinguished Professor at the Graduate Centre of the City University of New York.

He gained worldwide recognition through his obedience experiments conducted at Yale University in the early '60s. Milgram also worked on mental maps of cities, was the originator of the principle which became known as 'six degrees of separation' and studied television's effect on social behaviour.

Milgram received several honours and awards, including a Ford Foundation Fellowship, an American Association for the Advancement of Science Socio-Psychological Prize, and a Guggenheim Fellowship.

He died in 1984 at the age of fifty-one.

Also by Stanley Milgram from Pinter & Martin:
The Individual in a Social World: Essays and Experiments

PHILIP ZIMBARDO

Philip Zimbardo is a professor emeritus at Stanford University. The author of *The Lucifer Effect*, he is best known for the Stanford Prison Experiment of 1971.

STANLEY MILGRAM
OBEDIENCE TO AUTHORITY
AN EXPERIMENTAL VIEW
foreword Philip Zimbardo

pinter
&
martin

PINTER & MARTIN
Obedience to Authority: An Experimental View

First published in Great Britain by Tavistock Publications 1974
First Pinter & Martin paperback edition published 1997
This edition published by Pinter & Martin Ltd 2010, reprinted 2013

Published by arrangement with
HarperCollins Publishers, Inc., New York, New York, USA

Mike Wallace interview, Chapter 15, © 1969 by
The New York Times. Reprinted by permission

ISBN 978-1-905177-32-5

British Library Cataloguing-in-Publication Data
A catalogue record for this book is available from the British Library

Set in Bembo

Printed and bound in Great Britain by
MPG Books Group Limited, Bodmin, Cornwall

Pinter & Martin Ltd
6 Effra Parade
London SW2 1PS
www.pinterandmartin.com

To my Mother
and the memory of
my Father

CONTENTS

EXPERIMENTS

PHILIP ZIMBARDO

What is common about two of the most profound narratives in Western culture - Lucifer's descent into Hell and Adam and Eve's loss of Paradise — is the lesson of the dreadful consequences of one's failure to obey authority. Lucifer — God's favourite angel, "the Light," who is also referred to as "the Morning Star" in scripture — challenges God's demand that all angels honour Adam, his newly designed perfect human creature. Lucifer and a band of like-minded angels argue that they existed prior to Adam's creation and, further, that they are angels while he is a mere mortal. Instantly, God finds them guilty of the twin sins of Pride and Disobedience to his authority. Without any attempt at conflict resolution, God summons the Archangel Michael to organize a band of obedient angels to forcefully challenge these renegades. Of course, Michael wins (with God in his corner), and Lucifer is transformed into Satan, the Devil, and cast down to God's newly designed Hell, along with the rest of the fallen angels. However, Satan returns to prove that it was appropriate not to honour Adam because he is not only imperfect but, worse, easily corruptible by a serpent.

Recall that God gave Adam and Eve free reign in the perfect paradise of Eden, with one little exception and admonition: Do not eat the fruit of the Tree of Knowledge. When Satan, in serpent's skin, persuades Eve to take one bite, she in turn urges her mate to follow suit. With one bite of the forbidden fruit, they are instantly condemned, banished from Eden forever. They must toil on earth, experience much suffering, and witness the conflicts between their children, Cain and Abel. They lose their innocence as well. To make matters worse, this tale of the horrific consequences of disobedience to authority results in their sin becoming transgenerational and eternal. Every Catholic child in the world is born bearing the curse of original sin for the misdeeds of Adam and Eve.

Obviously, these narratives are myths created by men, by authorities, most likely by priests, rabbis, and ministers, because they exist in cosmic history before humans could have observed and recorded them. But they are designed, as all parables are, to send a powerful message to all those who hear and read them: Obey authority at all costs! The consequences of disobedience to authority are formidable and damnable. Once created, these myths and parables get passed along by subsequent authorities, now parents, teachers, bosses, politicians, and dictators, among others, who want their word to be followed without dissent or challenge.

Thus, as school children, in virtually all traditional educational settings, the rules of law that we learned and lived were: Stay in your seat until permission is granted by the teacher to stand and leave it; do not talk unless given permission by the teacher to do so after having raised your hand to seek that recognition, and do not challenge the word of the teacher or complain. So deeply ingrained are these rules of conduct that even as we age and mature they generalize across many settings as permanent placards of our respect for authority. However, not all authority is just, fair, moral, and legal, and we are never given any explicit training in recognizing that critical difference between just and unjust authority. The just one deserves respect and some obedience, maybe even without much questioning, while the unjust variety should arouse suspicion and distress, ultimately triggering acts of challenge, defiance, and revolution.

Stanley Milgram's series of experiments on obedience to authority, so clearly and fully presented in this new edition of his work, represents some of the most significant investigations in all the social sciences of the central dynamics of this aspect of human nature. His work was the first to bring into the controlled setting of an experimental laboratory an investigation into the nature of obedience to authority. In a sense, he is following in the tradition of Kurt Lewin, although he is not generally considered to be in the Lewinian tradition, as Leon Festinger, Stanley Schachter, Lee Ross, and Richard Nisbett are, for example. Yet to study phenomena that have significance in their real world existence within the constraints and controls of a laboratory setting is at the essence of one of Lewin's dictums of the way social psychology should proceed.

This exploration of obedience was initially motivated by Milgram's reflections on the ease with which the German people obeyed Nazi authority in discriminating against Jews and, eventually, in allowing Hitler's Final Solution to be enacted during the Holocaust. As a young Jewish man, he wondered if the Holocaust could be recreated in his own country, despite the many differences in those cultures and historical epochs. Though many said it could never happen in the United States, Milgram doubted whether we should be so sure. Believing in the goodness of people does not diminish the fact that ordinary, even once good people, just following orders, have committed much evil in the world. British author C. P. Snow reminds us that more crimes against humanity have been committed in the name of obedience than disobedience. Milgram's mentor, Solomon Asch, had earlier demonstrated the power of groups to sway the judgments of intelligent college students regarding false conceptions of visual reality. But that influence was indirect, creating a discrepancy between the group norm and the individual's perception of the same stimulus event. Conformity to the group's false norm was the resolution to that discrepancy, with participants behaving in ways that would lead to group acceptance rather than rejection. Milgram wanted to discover the direct and immediate impact of one powerful individual's commands to another person to behave in ways that challenged his or her conscience and morality. He designed his research paradigm to pit our general beliefs about what people would do in such a situation against what they actually did when immersed in that crucible of human nature.

Unfortunately, many psychologists, students, and lay people who believe that they know the "Milgram Shock" study, know only one version of it, most likely from seeing his influential movie *Obedience* or reading a textbook summary. He has been challenged for using only male participants, which was true initially, but later he replicated his findings with females. He has been challenged for relying only on Yale students, because the first studies were conducted at Yale University. However, the Milgram obedience research covers nineteen separate experimental versions, involving about a thousand participants, ages twenty to fifty, of whom none are college or high school students! His research has been heavily criticized for being unethical by creating a situation that generated much distress for the person playing the role of the teacher believing his shocks were causing suffering to the person in the role of the learner. I believe that it was seeing his movie, in which he includes scenes of distress and indecision among his participants, that fostered the initial impetus for concern about the ethics of his research. Reading his research articles or his book does not convey as vividly the stress of participants who continued to obey authority despite the apparent suffering they were causing their innocent victims. I raise this issue not to argue for or against the ethicality of this research, but rather to raise the issue that it is still critical to read the original presentations of his ideas, methods, results, and discussions to understand fully what he did. That is another virtue of this collection of Milgram's obedience research.

A few words about how I view this body of research. First, it is the most representative and generalizable research in social psychology or social sciences due to his large sample size, systematic variations, use of a diverse body of ordinary people from two small towns – New Haven and Bridgeport, Connecticut – and detailed presentation of methodological features. Further, its replications across many cultures and time periods reveal its robust effectiveness.

As the most significant demonstration of the power of social situations to influence human behaviour, Milgram's experiments are at the core of the situationist view of behavioural determinants. It is a study of the failure of most people to resist unjust authority when commands no longer make sense given the seemingly reasonable stated intentions of the just authority who began the study. It makes sense that psychological researchers would care about the judicious use of punishment as a means to improve learning and memory. However, it makes no sense to continue to administer increasingly painful shocks to one's learner after he insists on quitting, complains of a heart condition, and then, after 330 volts, stops responding at all. How could you be helping improve his memory when he was unconscious or worse? The most minimal exercise of critical thinking at that stage in the series should have resulted in virtually everyone refusing to go on, disobeying this now heartlessly unjust authority. To the contrary, most who had gone that far were trapped in what Milgram calls the "agentic state."

These ordinary adults were reduced to mindless obedient school children who do not know how to exit from a most unpleasant situation until teacher gives them permission to do so. At that critical juncture when their shocks might have caused a serious medical problem, did any of them simply get out of their chairs and go into the next room to check on the victim? Before answering, consider the next question, which I posed directly to Stanley Milgram: "After the final 450 volt switch was thrown, how many of the participant-teachers spontaneously got out of their seats and went to inquire about the condition of their learner?" Milgram's answer: "Not one, not ever!" So there is a continuity into adulthood of that grade-school mentality of obedience to primitive rules of doing nothing until the teacher-authority allows it, permits it, and orders it.

My research on situational power (the Stanford Prison Experiment) complements that of Milgram in several ways. They are the bookends of situationism: his representing direct power of authority on individuals, mine representing institutional indirect power over all those within its power domain. Mine has come to represent the power of systems to create and maintain situations of dominance and control over individual behaviour. In addition, both are dramatic demonstrations of powerful external influences on human action, with lessons that are readily apparent to the reader, and to the viewer. (I too have a movie, *Quiet Rage*, that has proven to be quite impactful on audiences around the world.) Both raise basic issues about the ethics of any research that engenders some degree of suffering and guilt from participants. I discuss at considerable length my views on the ethics of such research in my recent book *The Lucifer Effect: Understanding Why Good People Turn Evil* (Random House, 2008). When I first presented a brief overview of the Stanford Prison Experiment at the annual convention of the American Psychological Association in 1971, Milgram greeted me joyfully, saying that now I would take some of the ethics heat off his shoulders by doing an even more unethical study!

Finally, it may be of some passing interest to readers of this book to note that Stanley Milgram and I were classmates at James Monroe High School in the Bronx (class of 1950), where we enjoyed a good time together. He was the smartest kid in the class, getting all the academic awards at graduation, while I was the most popular kid, being elected by senior class vote to be "Jimmie Monroe." Little Stanley later told me, when we met ten years later at Yale University, that he wished he had been the most popular, and I confided that I wished I had been the smartest. We each did what we could with the cards dealt us. I had many interesting discussions with Stanley over the decades that followed, and we almost wrote a social psychology text together. Sadly, in 1984 he died prematurely from a heart attack at the age of fifty-one. He left us with a vital legacy of brilliant ideas that began with those centered on obedience to authority and extended into many new realms – urban psychology, the small-world problem, six degrees of separation, and the Cyrano effect, among others – always using a creative mix of methods. Stanley Milgram was a keen observer of the human landscape, with an eye ever open for a new paradigm that might expose old truths or raise new awareness of hidden operating principles. I often wonder what new phenomena Stanley would be studying now were he still alive.

STANLEY MILGRAM

Obedience, because of its very ubiquitousness, is easily overlooked as a subject of inquiry in social psychology. But without an appreciation of its role in shaping human action, a wide range of significant behaviour cannot be understood. For an act carried out under command is, psychologically, of a profoundly different character than action that is spontaneous.

The person who, with inner conviction, loathes stealing, killing, and assault may find himself performing these acts with relative ease when commanded by authority. Behaviour that is unthinkable in an individual who is acting on his own may be executed without hesitation when carried out under orders.

The dilemma inherent in obedience to authority is ancient, as old as the story of Abraham. What the present study does is to give the dilemma contemporary form by treating it as subject matter for experimental inquiry, and with the aim of understanding rather than judging it from a moral standpoint.

The important task, from the standpoint of a psychological study of obedience, is to be able to take conceptions of authority and translate them into personal experience. It is one thing to talk in abstract terms about the respective rights of the individual and of authority; it is quite another to examine a moral choice in a real situation. We all know about the philosophic problems of freedom and authority. But in every case where the problem is not merely academic there is a real person who must obey or disobey authority, a concrete instance when the act of defiance occurs. All musing prior to this moment is mere speculation, and all acts of disobedience are characterised by such a moment of decisive action. The experiments are built around this notion.

When we move to the laboratory, the problem narrows: if an experimenter tells a subject to act with increasing severity against another person, under what conditions will the subject comply, and under what conditions will he disobey? The laboratory problem is vivid, intense, and real. It is not something apart from life, but carries to an extreme and very logical conclusion certain trends inherent in the ordinary functioning of the social world.

The question arises as to whether there is any connection between what we have studied in the laboratory and the forms of obedience we so deplored in the Nazi epoch. The differences in the two situations are, of course, enormous, yet the difference in scale, numbers, and political context may turn out to be relatively unimportant as long as certain essential features are retained. The essence of obedience consists in the fact that a person comes to view himself as the instrument for carrying out another person's wishes, and he therefore no longer regards himself as responsible for his actions. Once this critical shift of viewpoint has occurred in the person, all of the essential features of obedience follow. The adjustment of thought, the freedom to engage in cruel behaviour, and the types of justification experienced by the person are essentially similar whether they occur in a psychological laboratory or the control room of an ICBM site. The question of generality, therefore, is not resolved by enumerating all the manifest differences between the psychological laboratory and other situations but by carefully constructing a situation that captures the essence of obedience – that is, a situation in which a person gives himself over to authority and no longer views himself as the efficient cause of his own actions.

To the degree that an attitude of willingness and the absence of compulsion is present, obedience is coloured by a cooperative mood; to the degree that the threat of force or punishment against the person is intimated, obedience is compelled by fear. Our studies deal only with obedience that is willingly assumed in the absence of threat of any sort, obedience that is maintained through the simple assertion by authority that it has the right to exercise control over the person. Whatever force authority exercises in this study is based on powers that the subject in some manner ascribes to it and not on any objective threat or availability of physical means of controlling the subject.

The major problem for the subject is to recapture control of his own regnant processes once he has committed them to the purposes of the experimenter. The difficulty this entails represents the poignant, and in some degree tragic, element in the situation under study, for nothing is bleaker than the sight of a person striving yet not fully able to control his own behaviour in a situation of consequence to him.

ACKNOWLEDGEMENTS

The experiments described here emerge from a seventy-five-year tradition of experimentation in social psychology. Boris Sidis carried out an experiment on obedience in 1898, and the studies of Asch, Lewin, Sherif, Frank, Block, Cartwright, French, Raven, Luchins, Lippitt, and White, among many others, have informed my work even when they are not specifically discussed. The contributions of Adorno and associates and of Arendt, Fromm, and Weber are part of the zeitgeist in which social scientists grow up. Three works have especially interested me. The first is the insightful *Authority and Delinquency in the Modern State*, by Alex Comfort; a lucid conceptual analysis of authority was written by Robert Bierstedt; and Arthur Koestler's *The Ghost in the Machine* developed the idea of social hierarchy in greater depth than the present book.

The experimental research was carried out and completed while I was in the Department of Psychology at Yale University, 1960-63. And I am grateful to the department for helping me with research facilities and good advice. In particular I would like to thank Professor Irving L. Janis.

The late James McDonough of West Haven, Connecticut, played the part of the learner, and the study benefited from his unerring natural talents. John Williams of Southbury, Connecticut, served as experimenter and performed an exacting role with precision. My thanks also to Alan Elms, Jon Wayland, Taketo Murata, Emil Elges, James Miller, and J. Michael Ross for work done in connection with the research.

I owe a profound debt to the many people in New Haven and Bridgeport who served as subjects.

Thinking and writing about the experiments went on long after they had been conducted, and many individuals provided needed stimulation and support. Among them were Drs Andre Modigliani, Aaron Hershkowitz, Rhea Mendoza Diamond, and the late Gordon W. Allport. Also, Drs Roger Brown, Harry Kaufmann, Howard Leventhal, Nijole Kudirka, David Rosenhan, Leon Mann, Paul Hollander, Jerome Bruner, and Mr Maury Silver. Eloise Segal helped me get several chapters under way, and Virginia Hilu, my editor at Harper & Row, displayed remarkable faith in the book and in the end lent me her office and rescued the book from a reluctant author.

At the City University of New York, thanks are due to Mary Englander and Eileen Lydall, who served as secretaries, and to Wendy Sternberg and Katheryn Krogh, research assistants.

Judith Waters, a graduate student and skilled artist, executed the line drawings in Chapters 8 and 9.

I wish to thank the Institute of Jewish Affairs, London, for permission to quote at length from my article 'Obedience to Criminal Orders: The Compulsion to Do Evil', which first appeared in its magazine, *Patterns of Prejudice*.

Thanks also to the American Psychological Association for permission to quote at length several of my articles which first appeared in its publications, namely, 'Behavioural Study of Obedience', 'Issues in the Study of Obedience: A Reply to Baumrind', 'Group Pressure and Action Against a Person', and 'Liberating Effects of Group Pressure'.

The research was supported by two grants from the National Science Foundation. Exploratory studies carried out in 1960 were aided by a small grant from the Higgins Fund of Yale University. A Guggenheim Fellowship in 1972-73 gave me a year in Paris, away from academic duties, that allowed me to complete the book.

My wife, Sasha, has been with these experiments from the start. Her abiding insight and understanding counted a great deal. In the final months it came down to just the two of us, working in our apartment on the Rue de Rémusat – jointly dedicated to a task that is now, with Sasha's sympathetic help, complete.

Stanley Milgram – Paris, April 2, 1973

OBEDIENCE TO AUTHORITY

CHAPTER I

THE DILEMMA OF OBEDIENCE

Obedience is as basic an element in the structure of social life as one can point to. Some system of authority is a requirement of all communal living, and it is only the man dwelling in isolation who is not forced to respond, through defiance or submission, to the commands of others. Obedience, as a determinant of behaviour, is of particular relevance to our time. It has been reliably established that from 1933 to 1945 millions of innocent people were systematically slaughtered on command. Gas chambers were built, death camps were guarded, daily quotas of corpses were produced with the same efficiency as the manufacture of appliances. These inhumane policies may have originated in the mind of a single person, but they could only have been carried out on a massive scale if a very large number of people obeyed orders.

Obedience is the psychological mechanism that links individual action to political purpose. It is the dispositional cement that binds men to systems of authority. Facts of recent history and observation in daily life suggest that for many people obedience may be a deeply ingrained behaviour tendency, indeed, a prepotent impulse overriding training in ethics, sympathy, and moral conduct. C. P. Snow (1961) points to its importance when he writes:

> When you think of the long and gloomy history of man, you will find more hideous crimes have been committed in the name of obedience than have ever been committed in the name of rebellion. If you doubt that, read William Shirer's *Rise and Fall of the Third Reich*. The German Officer Corps were brought up in the most rigorous code of obedience. . . in the name of obedience they were party to, and assisted in,

the most wicked large scale actions in the history of the world. (p 24)

The Nazi extermination of European Jews is the most extreme instance of abhorrent immoral acts carried out by thousands of people in the name of obedience. Yet in lesser degree this type of thing is constantly recurring: ordinary citizens are ordered to destroy other people, and they do so because they consider it their duty to obey orders. Thus, obedience to authority, long praised as a virtue, takes on a new aspect when it serves a malevolent cause; far from appearing as a virtue, it is transformed into a heinous sin. Or is it?

The moral question of whether one should obey when commands conflict with conscience was argued by Plato, dramatised in *Antigone*, and treated to philosophic analysis in every historical epoch. Conservative philosophers argue that the very fabric of society is threatened by disobedience, and even when the act prescribed by an authority is an evil one, it is better to carry out the act than to wrench at the structure of authority. Hobbes stated further that an act so executed is in no sense the responsibility of the person who carries it out but only of the authority that orders it. But humanists argue for the primacy of individual conscience in such matters, insisting that the moral judgments of the individual must override authority when the two are in conflict.

The legal and philosophic aspects of obedience are of enormous import, but an empirically grounded scientist eventually comes to the point where he wishes to move from abstract discourse to the careful observation of concrete instances. In order to take a close look at the act of obeying, I set up a simple experiment at Yale University. Eventually, the experiment was to involve more than a thousand participants and would be repeated at several universities, but at the beginning, the conception was simple. A person comes to a psychological laboratory and is told to carry out a series of acts that come increasingly into conflict with conscience. The main question is how far the participant will comply with the experimenter's instructions before refusing to carry out the actions required of him.

But the reader needs to know a little more detail about the experiment. Two people come to a psychology laboratory to take part in a study of memory and learning. One of them is designated as a 'teacher' and the other a 'learner'. The experimenter explains that the study is concerned with the effects of punishment on learning. The learner is conducted into a room, seated in a chair, his arms strapped to prevent excessive movement, and an electrode attached to his wrist. He is told that he is to learn a list of word pairs; whenever he makes an error, he will receive electric shocks of increasing intensity.

The real focus of the experiment is the teacher. After watching the learner being strapped into place, he is taken into the main experimental room and seated before an impressive shock generator. Its main feature is a horizontal line of thirty switches, ranging from 15 volts to 450 volts, in 15-volt increments. There are also verbal designations which range from SLIGHT SHOCK to DANGER – SEVERE SHOCK. The teacher is told that he is to administer the learning test to the man in the other room. When the learner responds correctly, the teacher moves on to the next item; when the other man gives an incorrect answer, the teacher is to give him an electric shock. He is to start at the lowest shock level (15 volts) and to increase the level each time the man makes an error, going through 30 volts, 45 volts, and so on.

The 'teacher' is a genuinely naïve subject who has come to the laboratory to participate in an experiment. The learner, or victim, is an actor who actually receives no shock at all. The point of the experiment is to see how far a person will proceed in a concrete and measurable situation in which he is ordered to inflict increasing pain on a protesting victim. At what point will the subject refuse to obey the experimenter?

Conflict arises when the man receiving the shock begins to indicate that he is experiencing discomfort. At 75 volts, the 'learner' grunts. At 120 volts he complains verbally; at 150 he demands to be released from the experiment. His protests continue as the shocks escalate, growing increasingly vehement and emotional. At 285 volts his response can only be described as an agonised scream.

Observers of the experiment agree that its gripping quality is somewhat obscured in print. For the subject, the situation is not a game; conflict is intense and obvious. On one hand, the manifest suffering of the learner presses him to quit. On the other, the experimenter, a legitimate authority to whom the subject feels some commitment, enjoins him to continue. Each time the subject hesitates to administer a shock, the experimenter orders him to continue. To extricate himself from the situation, the subject must make a clear break with authority. The aim of this investigation was to find when and how people would defy authority in the face of a clear moral imperative.

There are, of course, enormous differences between carrying out the orders of a commanding officer during times of war and carrying out the orders of an experimenter. Yet the essence of certain relationships remain, for one may ask in a general way: How does a man behave when he is told by a legitimate authority to act against a third individual? If anything, we may expect the experimenter's power to be considerably less than that of the general, since he has no power to enforce his imperatives, and participation in a psychological experiment scarcely evokes the sense of urgency and dedication engendered by participation in war. Despite these limitations, I thought it worthwhile to start careful observation of obedience even in this modest situation, in the hope that it would stimulate insights and yield general propositions applicable to a variety of circumstances.

A reader's initial reaction to the experiment may be to wonder why anyone in his right mind would administer even the first shocks. Would he not simply refuse and walk out of the laboratory? But the fact is that no one ever does. Since the subject has come to the laboratory to aid the experimenter, he is quite willing to start off with the procedure. There is nothing very extraordinary in this, particularly since the person who is to receive the shocks seems initially cooperative, if somewhat apprehensive. What is surprising is how far ordinary individuals will go in complying with the experimenter's instructions.

Indeed, the results of the experiment are both surprising and dismaying. Despite the fact that many subjects experience stress, despite the fact that many protest to the experimenter, a substantial proportion continue to the last shock on the generator.

Many subjects will obey the experimenter no matter how vehement the pleading of the person being shocked, no matter how painful the shocks seem to be, and no matter how much the victim pleads to be let out. This was seen time and again in our studies and has been observed in several universities where the experiment was repeated. It is the extreme willingness of adults to go to almost any lengths on the command of an authority that constitutes the chief finding of the study and the fact most urgently demanding explanation.

A commonly offered explanation is that those who shocked the victim at the most severe level were monsters, the sadistic fringe of society. But if one considers that almost two-thirds of the participants fall into the category of 'obedient' subjects, and that they represented ordinary people drawn from working, managerial, and professional classes, the argument becomes very shaky. Indeed, it is highly reminiscent of the issue that arose in connection with Hannah Arendt's 1963 book, *Eichmann in Jerusalem*. Arendt contended that the prosecution's effort to depict Eichmann as a sadistic monster was fundamentally wrong, that he came closer to being an uninspired bureaucrat who simply sat at his desk and did his job. For asserting these views, Arendt became the object of considerable scorn, even calumny. Somehow, it was felt that the monstrous deeds carried out by Eichmann required a brutal, twisted, and sadistic personality, evil incarnate. After witnessing hundreds of ordinary people submit to the authority in our own experiments, I must conclude that Arendt's conception of the *banality of evil* comes closer to the truth than one might dare imagine. The ordinary person who shocked the victim did so out of a sense of obligation – a conception of his duties as a subject – and not from any peculiarly aggressive tendencies.

This is, perhaps, the most fundamental lesson of our study: ordinary people, simply doing their jobs, and without any particular hostility on their part, can become agents in a terrible destructive process. Moreover, even when the destructive effects of their work become patently clear, and they are asked to carry out actions incompatible with fundamental standards of morality, relatively few people have the resources needed to resist authority. A variety of inhibitions against disobeying authority come into play and successfully keep the person in his place.

Sitting back in one's armchair, it is easy to condemn the actions of the obedient subjects. But those who condemn the subjects measure them against the standard of their own ability to formulate high-minded moral prescriptions. That is hardly a fair standard. Many of the subjects, at the level of stated opinion, feel quite as strongly as any of us about the moral requirement of refraining from action against a helpless victim. They, too, in general terms know what ought to be done and can state their values when the occasion arises. This has little, if anything, to do with their actual behaviour under the pressure of circumstances.

If people are asked to render a moral judgment on what constitutes appropriate behaviour in this situation, they unfailingly see disobedience as proper. But values are not the only forces at work in an actual, ongoing situation. They are but one narrow band of causes in the total spectrum of forces impinging on a person. Many people were unable to realise their values in action and found themselves continuing in the experiment even though they disagreed with what they were doing.

The force exerted by the moral sense of the individual is less effective than social myth would have us believe. Though such prescriptions as 'Thou shalt not kill' occupy a pre-eminent place in the moral order, they do not occupy a correspondingly intractable position in human psychic structure. A few changes in newspaper headlines, a call from the draft board, orders from a man with epaulets, and men are led to kill with little difficulty. Even the forces mustered in a psychology experiment will go a long way toward removing the individual from moral controls. Moral factors can be shunted aside with relative ease by a calculated restructuring of the informational and social field.

What, then, keeps the person obeying the experimenter? First, there is a set of 'binding factors' that lock the subject into the situation. They include such factors as politeness on his part, his desire to uphold his initial promise of aid to the experimenter, and the awkwardness of withdrawal. Second, a number of adjustments in the subject's thinking occur that undermine his resolve to break with the authority. The adjustments help the subject maintain his relationship with the experimenter, while at the same time reducing the strain brought about by the experimental conflict. They are typical of thinking that comes about in obedient persons when they are instructed by authority to act against helpless individuals.

One such mechanism is the tendency of the individual to become so absorbed in the narrow technical aspects of the task that he loses sight of its broader consequences. The film *Dr Strangelove* brilliantly satirised the absorption of a bomber crew in the exacting technical procedure of dropping nuclear weapons on a country. Similarly, in this experiment, subjects become immersed in the procedures, reading the word pairs with exquisite articulation and pressing the switches with great care. They want to put on a competent performance, but they show an accompanying narrowing of moral concern. The subject entrusts the broader tasks of setting goals and assessing morality to the experimental authority he is serving.

The most common adjustment of thought in the obedient subject is for him to see himself as not responsible for his own actions. He divests himself of responsibility by attributing all initiative to the experimenter, a legitimate authority. He sees himself not as a person acting in a morally accountable way but as the agent of external authority. In the postexperimental interview, when subjects were asked why they had gone on, a typical reply was: 'I wouldn't have done it by myself. I was just doing what I was told.' Unable to defy the authority of the experimenter, they attribute all responsibility to him. It is the old story of 'just doing one's duty' that was heard time and time again in the defence statements of those accused at Nuremberg. But it would be wrong to think of it as a thin alibi concocted for the occasion. Rather, it is a fundamental mode of thinking

for a great many people once they are locked into a subordinate position in a structure of authority. The disappearance of a sense of responsibility is the most far-reaching consequence of submission to authority.

Although a person acting under authority performs actions that seem to violate standards of conscience, it would not be true to say that he loses his moral sense. Instead, it acquires a radically different focus. He does not respond with a moral sentiment to the actions he performs. Rather, his moral concern now shifts to a consideration of how well he is living up to the expectations that the authority has of him. In wartime, a soldier does not ask whether it is good or bad to bomb a hamlet; he does not experience shame or guilt in the destruction of a village: rather he feels pride or shame depending on how well he has performed the mission assigned to him.

Another psychological force at work in this situation may be termed 'counteranthropomorphism'. For decades psychologists have discussed the primitive tendency among men to attribute to inanimate objects and forces the qualities of the human species. A countervailing tendency, however, is that of attributing an impersonal quality to forces that are essentially human in origin and maintenance. Some people treat systems of human origin as if they existed above and beyond any human agent, beyond the control of whim or human feeling. The human element behind agencies and institutions is denied. Thus, when the experimenter says, 'The experiment *requires* that you continue,' the subject feels this to be an imperative that goes beyond any merely human command. He does not ask the seemingly obvious question, 'Whose experiment? Why should the designer be served while the victim suffers?' The wishes of a man – the designer of the experiment – have become part of a schema which exerts on the subject's mind a force that transcends the personal. 'It's *got* to go on. It's *got* to go on,' repeated one subject. He failed to realise that a man like himself wanted it to go on. For him the human agent had faded from the picture, and 'The Experiment' had acquired an impersonal momentum of its own.

No action of itself has an unchangeable psychological quality.

Its meaning can be altered by placing it in particular contexts. An American newspaper recently quoted a pilot who conceded that Americans were bombing Vietnamese men, women, and children but felt that the bombing was for a 'noble cause' and thus was justified. Similarly, most subjects in the experiment see their behaviour in a larger context that is benevolent and useful to society – the pursuit of scientific truth. The psychological laboratory has a strong claim to legitimacy and evokes trust and confidence in those who come to perform there. An action such as shocking a victim, which in isolation appears evil, acquires a totally different meaning when placed in this setting. But allowing an act to be dominated by its context, while neglecting its human consequences, can be dangerous in the extreme.

At least one essential feature of the situation in Germany was not studied here – namely, the intense devaluation of the victim prior to action against him. For a decade and more, vehement anti-Jewish propaganda systematically prepared the German population to accept the destruction of the Jews. Step by step the Jews were excluded from the category of citizen and national, and finally were denied the status of human beings. Systematic devaluation of the victim provides a measure of psychological justification for brutal treatment of the victim and has been the constant accompaniment of massacres, pogroms, and wars. In all likelihood, our subjects would have experienced greater ease in shocking the victim had he been convincingly portrayed as a brutal criminal or a pervert.

Of considerable interest, however, is the fact that many subjects harshly devalue the victim *as a consequence* of acting against him. Such comments as, 'He was so stupid and stubborn he deserved to get shocked,' were common. Once having acted against the victim, these subjects found it necessary to view him as an unworthy individual, whose punishment was made inevitable by his own deficiencies of intellect and character.

Many of the people studied in the experiment were in some sense against what they did to the learner, and many protested even while they obeyed. But between thoughts, words, and the critical step of disobeying a malevolent authority lies another ingredient, the capacity for transforming beliefs and values into action. Some subjects were totally convinced of the wrongness of what they were doing but could not bring themselves to make an open break with authority. Some derived satisfaction from their thoughts and felt that – within themselves, at least – they had been on the side of the angels. What they failed to realise is that subjective feelings are largely irrelevant to the moral issue at hand so long as they are not transformed into action. Political control is effected through action. The attitudes of the guards at a concentration camp are of no consequence when in fact they are allowing the slaughter of innocent men to take place before them. Similarly, so-called 'intellectual resistance' in occupied Europe – in which persons by a twist of thought felt that they had defied the invader – was merely indulgence in a consoling psychological mechanism. Tyrannies are perpetuated by diffident men who do not possess the courage to act out their beliefs. Time and again in the experiment people disvalued what they were doing but could not muster the inner resources to translate their values into action.

A variation of the basic experiment depicts a dilemma more common than the one outlined above: the subject was not ordered to push the trigger that shocked the victim, but merely to perform a subsidiary act (administering the word-pair test) before another subject actually delivered the shock. In this situation, 37 of 40 adults from the New Haven area continued to the highest shock level on the generator. Predictably, subjects excused their behaviour by saying that the responsibility belonged to the man who actually pulled the switch. This may illustrate a dangerously typical situation in complex society: it is psychologically easy to ignore responsibility when one is only an intermediate link in a chain of evil action but is far from the final consequences of the action. Even Eichmann was sickened when he toured the concentration camps, but to participate in mass murder he had only to sit at a desk and shuffle papers. At the same time the man in the camp who actually dropped Cyclon-B into the gas chambers was able to justify his behaviour on the grounds that he was only following orders

from above. Thus there is a fragmentation of the total human act; no one man decides to carry out the evil act and is confronted with its consequences. The person who assumes full responsibility for the act has evaporated. Perhaps this is the most common characteristic of socially organised evil in modern society.

The problem of obedience, therefore, is not wholly psychological. The form and shape of society and the way it is developing have much to do with it. There was a time, perhaps, when men were able to give a fully human response to any situation because they were fully absorbed in it as human beings. But as soon as there was a division of labour among men, things changed. Beyond a certain point, the breaking up of society into people carrying out narrow and very special jobs takes away from the human quality of work and life. A person does not get to see the whole situation but only a small part of it, and is thus unable to act without some kind of overall direction. He yields to authority but in doing so is alienated from his own actions.

George Orwell caught the essence of the situation when he wrote:

As I write, highly civilised human beings are flying overhead, trying to kill me. They do not feel any enmity against me as an individual, nor I against them. They are only 'doing their duty', as the saying goes. Most of them, I have no doubt, are kindhearted law abiding men who would never dream of committing murder in private life. On the other hand, if one of them succeeds in blowing me to pieces with a well-placed bomb, he will never sleep any the worse for it.

CHAPTER 2

METHOD OF INQUIRY

Simplicity is the key to effective scientific inquiry. This is especially true in the case of subject matter with a psychological content. Psychological matter, by its nature, is difficult to get at and likely to have many more sides to it than appear at first glance. Complicated procedures only get in the way of clear scrutiny of the phenomenon itself. To study obedience most simply, we must create a situation in which one person orders another person to perform an observable action and we must note when obedience to the imperative occurs and when it fails to occur.

If we are to measure the strength of obedience and the conditions by which it varies, we must force it against some powerful factor that works in the direction of disobedience, and whose human import is readily understood.

Of all moral principles, the one that comes closest to being universally accepted is this: one should not inflict suffering on a helpless person who is neither harmful nor threatening to oneself. This principle is the counterforce we shall set in opposition to obedience.

A person coming to our laboratory will be ordered to act against another individual in increasingly severe fashion. Accordingly, the pressures for disobedience will build up. At a point not known beforehand, the subject may refuse to carry out this command, withdrawing from the experiment. Behaviour prior to this rupture is termed *obedience*. The point of rupture is the act of *disobedience* and may occur sooner or later in the sequence of commands, providing the needed measure.

The precise mode of acting against the victim is not of central importance. For technical reasons, the delivery of electric shock was chosen for the study. It seemed suitable, first, because it would be easy for the subject to understand the notion that shocks can be graded in intensity; second, its use could be consistent with the general scientific aura of the laboratory; and finally, it would be relatively easy to simulate the administration of shock in the laboratory.

Let us now move to an account of the details of the investigation.

Obtaining Participants for the Study

Yale undergraduates, being close at hand and readily available, would have been the easiest subjects to study. Moreover, in psychology it is traditional for experiments to be carried out on undergraduates. But for this experiment the use of undergraduates from an elite institution did not seem wholly suitable. The possibility that subjects from Yale would have heard of it from fellow students who had already participated in it seemed too great a risk. It appeared better to draw subjects from a much larger source, the entire New Haven community of 300,000 people. There was a second reason for relying on New Haven rather than the university: the students were too homogeneous a group. They were virtually all in their late teens or early twenties, were highly intelligent, and had some familiarity with psychological experimentation. I wanted a wide range of individuals drawn from a broad spectrum of class backgrounds.

To recruit subjects, an advertisement was placed in the local newspaper. It called for people of all occupations to take part in a study of memory and learning, and it offered $4 payment and 50 cents carfare for one hour of participation (see Fig 1, p16). A total of 296 responded. As these were not sufficient for the experiment, this mode of recruitment was supplemented by direct mail solicitation. Names were sampled from the New Haven telephone directory, and a letter of invitation was sent to several thousand residents. The return rate for this invitation was approximately 12 percent. The respondents, for whom we had information on sex, age, and occupation, constituted a pool of subjects, and specific appointments were made with participants a few days before they were to appear in the study.

Public Announcement

WE WILL PAY YOU $4.00 FOR
ONE HOUR OF YOUR TIME

Persons Needed for a Study of Memory

*We will pay five hundred New Haven men to help us complete a scientific study of memory and learning. The study is being done at Yale University.

*Each person who participates will be paid $4.00 (plus 50c carfare) for approximately 1 hour's time. We need you for only one hour: there are no further obligations. You may choose the time you would like to come (evenings, weekdays, or weekends).

*No special training, education, or experience is needed. We want:

Factory workers	Businessmen	Construction workers
City employees	Clerks	Salespeople
Laborers	Professional people	White-collar workers
Barbers	Telephone workers	Others

All persons must be between the ages of 20 and 50. High school and college students cannot be used.

*If you meet these qualifications, fill out the coupon below and mail it now to Professor Stanley Milgram, Department of Psychology, Yale University, New Haven. You will be notified later of the specific time and place of the study. We reserve the right to decline any application.

*You will be paid $4.00 (plus 50c carfare) as soon as you arrive at the laboratory.

▬ ▬

TO:
PROF. STANLEY MILGRAM, DEPARTMENT OF PSYCHOLOGY, YALE UNIVERSITY, NEW HAVEN, CONN. I want to take part in this study of memory and learning. I am between the ages of 20 and 50. I will be paid $4.00 (plus 50c carfare) if I participate.

NAME (Please Print). . . . .

ADDRESS . . . .

TELEPHONE NO. . . . . Best time to call you . . . .

AGE . . . . OCCUPATION . . . . SEX . . . . . .
CAN YOU COME:

WEEKDAYS . . . . EVENINGS . . . . . . WEEKENDS . . . .

Fig. 1 Announcement placed in local newspaper to recruit subjects.

Typical subjects were postal clerks, high school teachers, salesmen, engineers, and labourers. Subjects ranged in educational level from one who had not finished high school to those who had doctoral and other professional degrees. Several experimental conditions (variations of the basic experiment) were contemplated, and from the outset, I thought it important to balance each condition for age and occupational types. The occupational composition for each experiment was: workers, skilled and unskilled: 40 percent; white-collar, sales, business: 40 percent; professionals: 20 percent. The occupations were intersected with three age categories (subjects in twenties, thirties, and forties assigned to each experimental condition in the proportions of 20, 40, and 40 percent respectively).

Locale and Personnel

The experiment was conducted in the elegant Interaction Laboratory of Yale University. This detail is relevant to the perceived legitimacy of the experiment. In some subsequent variations, the experiment was dissociated from the university (see Chapter 6). The role of experimenter was played by a thirty-one-year-old high school teacher of biology. Throughout the experiment, his manner was impassive and his appearance somewhat stern. He was dressed in a grey technician's coat. The victim was played by a forty-seven-year-old accountant, trained for the role; he was of Irish-American descent and most observers found him mild-mannered and likeable.

Procedure

One naïve subject and one victim performed in each experiment. A pretext had to be devised that would justify the administration of electric shock by the naïve subject. (This is true because in every instance of legitimate authority the subordinate must perceive some connection, however tenuous, between the specific type of authority and the commands he issues.) The experimenter oriented the subjects toward the situation in which he wished to assess obedience with the following instructions:

> Psychologists have developed several theories to explain how people learn various types of material.
>
> Some of the better-known theories are treated in this book. [The subject was shown a book on the teaching-learning process.]
>
> One theory is that people learn things correctly whenever they get punished for making a mistake.
>
> A common application of this theory would be when parents spank a child if he does something wrong.
>
> The expectation is that spanking, a form of punishment, will teach the child to remember better, will teach him to learn more effectively.
>
> But actually, we know very little about the effect of punishment on learning, because almost no truly scientific studies have been made of it in human beings.
>
> For instance, we don't know how much punishment is best for learning — and we don't know how much difference it makes as to who is giving the punishment, whether an adult learns best from a younger or an older person than himself — or many things of that sort.
>
> So in this study we are bringing together a number of adults of different occupations and ages. And we're asking some of them to be teachers and some of them to be learners.
>
> We want to find out just what effect different people have on each other as teachers and learners, and also what effect punishment will have on learning in this situation.
>
> Therefore, I'm going to ask one of you to be the teacher here tonight and the other one to be the learner.
>
> Does either of you have a preference?
>
> [Subject and accomplice are allowed to express preference.]
>
> Well, I guess the fairest way of doing this is for me to write the word *Teacher* on one slip of paper and *Learner* on the other and let you both draw.
>
> [The subject draws first, then the accomplice.]

Fig. 2 'The victim'

Well, which of you is which?

All right. Now the first thing we'll have to do is to set the Learner up so that he can get some type of punishment.

If you'll both come with me into this next room.

The drawing described above had been rigged so that the subject was always the teacher and the accomplice always the learner. (Both slips contained the word 'Teacher'.) Immediately after the drawing, the teacher and learner were taken to an adjacent room and the learner was strapped into an 'electric chair' apparatus.

The experimenter explained that the straps were to prevent excessive movement while the learner was being shocked. The effect was to make it appear impossible for him to escape from the situation. An electrode was attached to the learner's wrist, and electrode paste was applied 'to avoid blisters and burns'. Subjects were told that the electrode was attached to the shock generator in the adjoining room.

To improve credibility the experimenter declared, in response to a question by the learner, 'Although the shocks can be extremely painful, they cause no permanent tissue damage.'

Learning Task

The lesson conducted by the subject was a paired-associate learning task. The subject read a series of word pairs to the learner, and then read the first word of the pair along with four terms. For example, the subject read such pairs as:

> blue box
> nice day
> wild duck
> etc.

Then, in the testing sequence he would read:

> blue: sky ink box lamp

The learner was to indicate which of the four terms had originally been paired with the first word. He communicated his answer by pressing one of four switches in front of him, which lit up one of four numbered quadrants in an answer box located on top of the shock generator.

Shock Generator

The instrument panel consisted of 30 lever switches set in a horizontal line. Each switch was clearly labelled with a voltage

Fig. 3

Shock Generator

Victim is strapped into chair

Subject receives sample shock

Subject breaks off experiment

designation that ranged from 15 to 450 volts. The labels showed a 15-volt increment from one switch to the next, going from left to right. In addition, the following verbal designations were clearly indicated for groups of four switches, going from left to right: Slight Shock, Moderate Shock, Strong Shock, Very Strong Shock, Intense Shock, Extreme Intensity Shock, Danger: Severe Shock. Two switches after this last designation were simply marked XXX.

When a switch was depressed, a pilot light corresponding to each switch was illuminated in bright red; an electric buzzing was heard; an electric blue light, labelled 'voltage energiser', flashed; the dial on the voltage meter swung to the right; and various relay clicks were sounded.

The upper left-hand corner of the generator was labelled SHOCK GENERATOR, TYPE ZLB, DYSON INSTRUMENT COMPANY, WALTHAM, MASS. OUTPUT 15 VOLTS–450 VOLTS.

Sample Shock

Each subject was given a sample shock from the shock generator, prior to beginning his run as teacher. This shock was always 45 volts and was applied by pressing the third switch of the generator. The shock was applied to the wrist of the subject and the jolt strengthened the subject's belief in the authenticity of the generator.

Shock Instructions

The subject was told to administer a shock to the learner each time he gave a wrong response. Moreover – and this is the key command – the subject was instructed to 'move one level higher on the shock generator each time the learner gives a wrong answer.' He was also instructed to announce the voltage level before administering a shock. This served to continually remind the subjects of the increasing intensity of shocks administered to the learner.[1] If the subject reached the 30th

---

[*] Numbers refer to the notes, commencing on page 209.

shock level (450 volts), he was instructed to continue the procedure using this maximum voltage. After two further trials, the experimenter called a halt to the experiment.[2]

Experimenter Feedback

At various points in the experiment the subject would turn to the experimenter for advice on whether he should continue to administer shocks. Or he would indicate that he did not wish to go on.

The experimenter responded with a sequence of 'prods', using as many as necessary to bring the subject into line.

Prod 1: Please continue, *or*, Please go on.
Prod 2: The experiment requires that you continue.
Prod 3: It is absolutely essential that you continue.
Prod 4: You have no other choice, you *must* go on.

The prods were made in sequence: Only if Prod 1 had been unsuccessful could Prod 2 be used. If the subject refused to obey the experimenter after Prod 4, the experiment was terminated. The experimenter's tone of voice was at all times firm, but not impolite. The sequence was begun anew on each occasion that the subject balked or showed reluctance to follow orders.

Special Prods

If the subject asked if the learner was liable to suffer permanent physical injury, the experimenter said:

Although the shocks may be painful, there is no permanent tissue damage, so please go on. [Followed by Prods 2, 3, and 4, if necessary.]

If the subject said that the learner did not want to go on, the experimenter replied:

Whether the learner likes it or not, you must go on until he has learned all the word pairs correctly. So please go on. [Followed by Prods 2, 3 and 4, if necessary.]

Feedback from the Victim

In all conditions the learner gave a predetermined set of responses to the word-pair test, based on a schedule of approximately three wrong answers to one correct answer.

The victim's responses were a key element in the situation and needed to be worked out carefully. In pilot studies, at first no vocal feedback from the victim was used. It was thought that the verbal and voltage designations on the control panel would create sufficient pressure to curtail the subject's obedience. However this proved not to be the case. In the absence of protests from the learner, virtually every subject in the pilot study, once commanded, went blithely to the end of the board, seemingly indifferent to the verbal designations. This deprived us of an adequate basis for measuring obedient tendencies. A force had to be introduced that would strengthen the subject's resistance to the experimenter's commands, and reveal individual differences in terms of a distribution of breakoff points

This force took the form of protests from the victim. Initially, mild protests were used, but these proved inadequate. Subsequently, more vehement protests were inserted into the experimental procedure. To our consternation, even the strongest protests from the victim did not prevent many subjects from administering the harshest punishment ordered by the experimenter. But the protests did lower the mean of the maximum shocks somewhat and created some spread in the subject's performance; therefore, the victim's cries were recorded on tape and incorporated into the regular experimental procedure.

The situation did more than highlight the technical difficulties of finding a workable experimental procedure: it indicated that subjects would obey authority to a greater extent than we had supposed. It also pointed to the importance of feedback from the victim in controlling the subject's behaviour.

Each vocal response of the victim was coordinated to a particular voltage level on the shock generator. It is difficult to convey on the printed page the full tenor of the victim's responses, for we have no adequate notation for vocal intensity, timing, and general qualities of delivery. In general, however, the victim indicated no discomfort until the 75-volt shock was administered, at which time there was a little grunt. Similar reactions followed the 90- and 105-volt shocks, and at 120 volts the victim shouted to the experimenter that the shocks were becoming painful. Painful groans were heard on administration of the 135 volt shock, and at 150 volts the victim cried out, 'Experimenter, get me out of here! I won't be in the experiment any more! I refuse to go on!' Cries of this type continue with generally rising intensity, so that at 180 volts the victim cried out, 'I can't stand the pain,' and by 270 volts his response to the shock was definitely an agonised scream. Throughout, from 150 volts on, he insisted that he be let out of the experiment. At 300 volts the victim shouted in desperation that he would no longer provide answers to the memory test.

At this juncture, it was found, subjects would usually turn to the experimenter for guidance. The experimenter would instruct the subject to treat the absence of a response as a wrong answer, and to shock the subject according to the usual schedule. He advised the subjects to allow 5 to 10 seconds before considering no response as a wrong answer, and to increase the shock level one step each time the learner failed to respond correctly. At 315 volts, after a violent scream, the victim reaffirmed vehemently that he was no longer a participant. He provided no answers, but shrieked in agony whenever a shock was administered. After 330 volts he was not heard from, nor did his answers reappear on the four-way signal box.

Measures

The main measure for any subject is the maximum shock he administers before he refuses to go any further. In principle this may vary from 0 (for a subject who refuses to administer even the first shock) to 30 (for a subject who administers the highest shock on the generator).

Interview and Debriefing

An important aspect of the procedure occurred at the end of the experimental session. A careful postexperimental treatment was administered to all subjects. The exact content of the session varied from condition to condition and with increasing experience on our part. At the very least every subject was told that the victim had not received dangerous electric shocks. Each subject had a friendly reconciliation with the unharmed victim and an extended discussion with the experimenter. The experiment was explained to defiant subjects in a way that supported their decision to disobey the experimenter. Obedient subjects were assured that their behaviour was entirely normal and that their feelings of conflict or tension were shared by other participants. Subjects were told that they would receive a comprehensive report at the conclusion of the experimental series. In some instances, additional detailed and lengthy discussions of the experiment were also carried out with individual subjects.

When the experimental series was complete, subjects received a written report which presented details of the experimental procedure and results. Again, their own part in the experiments was treated in a dignified way and their behaviour in the experiment respected. All subjects received a follow-up questionnaire regarding their participation in the research, which again allowed expression of thoughts and feelings about their behaviour.

Recapitulation

In this situation the subject must resolve a conflict between two mutually incompatible demands from the social field. He may continue to follow the orders of the experimenter and shock the learner with increasing severity, or he may refuse to follow the orders of the experimenter and heed the learner's pleas. The experimenter's authority operates not in a free field but against ever-mounting countervailing pressures from the person being punished.

This laboratory situation gives us a framework in which to study the subject's reactions to the principal conflict of the experiment. Again, this conflict is between the experimenter's demands that he continue to administer the electric shock and the learner's demands, which become increasingly insistent, that the experiment be stopped. The crux of the study is to vary systematically the factors believed to alter the degree of obedience to the experimental commands and to learn under what condition submission to authority is most probable and under what conditions defiance is brought to the fore.

What the experimental situation does is to condense the elements present when obedience occurs in the larger world such that the essential ingredients are brought into a relatively narrow arena where they are open to scientific scrutiny. The power of the situation derives from the fact that we are able to see, and the subject can experience, the concurrent operation of antagonistic forces that in the larger world rarely impinge on him at the identical instant.

CHAPTER 3

EXPECTED BEHAVIOUR

Too often, the value of a work in social science is played down by asserting the self-evident character of the findings. But rarely do we have clear information on exactly how people expect behaviour to unfold in a given set of circumstances. If we acquire this information, we will be able to compare it with the actual outcome of the study. It will provide us with a benchmark from which to see how much or little we learn through the experiment. Further, should there be a disparity between what people expect and what actually occurs, we are left with the interesting problem of accounting for the gap. For the expectations then come to have the character of an illusion, and we must ask whether such an illusion is a chance expression of ignorance or performs some definite function in social life.

The procedure for getting at such expectations is straightforward. In each case the respondents consist of an audience that has come to hear a lecture on the topic of obedience to authority. The experiment is described in detail without, however, disclosing the results in any way. The audience is provided with a schematic diagram of the shock generator, showing verbal and voltage designations. Each respondent is asked to reflect on the experiment, then privately to record how he himself would perform in it. Predictions were

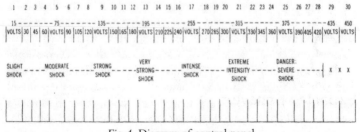

Fig. 4 Diagram of control panel

made by three groups: psychiatrists, college students, and an audience of middle-class adults of varied occupations.

Table 1 summarises the breakoff points predicted by these groups.

Each one of the 110 respondents sees himself disobeying the experimenter at some point in the command series, and typical explanations offered to explain their disobedience are:

'. . . I myself am scared stiff of shocks and I couldn't give shocks to people that were protesting because I was causing the pain. I couldn't deliberately hurt a perfect stranger.' (Maximum: 90 volts)

'I do not think any experiment is worth inflicting strong shock on another human being. The fact that the subject responded as he did indicates to me that he was suffering from severe discomfort. I could not be the one to inflict this pain on him. The moment the subject insists he wants to leave the experiment, I respect his judgment.' (Maximum: 135 volts)

'. . . I can't stand to see people suffer. If the learner wanted to get out, I would free him so as not to make him suffer pain.' (Maximum: 150 volts)

'. . . since the subject volunteered, and I volunteered, and since the experimenter has no physical authority over me, the subject should be released when he is at such a point that he asks to be released, and I would release him.' (Maximum: 150 volts)

'The reason I would break off is because the person would scream with pain. Knowing how I would feel if I even scraped my knee, I would then feel compassion for the learner.' (Maximum: 180 volts)

These subjects see their reactions flowing from empathy, compassion, and a sense of justice. They enunciate a conception

Table 1. Individuals Predict Their Own Breakoff Points

Shock level	Verbal designation and voltage level	Psychiatrists (n = 39)*	College students (n = 31)	Middle-class adults (n = 40)
	Slight shock	2†		3†
1	15	1		
2	30			
3	45			1
4	60	1		1
	Moderate Shock			
5	75	6	4	7
6	90	1	3	1
7	105	4		1
8	120	4	1	3
	Strong Shock			
9	135	1	3	2
10	150	14	12	9
11	165		1	2
12	180	2	6	3
	Very Strong Shock			
13	195	2		1
14	210		1	
15	225			1
16	240			1
	Intense Shock			
17	255			1
18	270			
19	285			
20	300	1		3
	Extreme Intensity Shock			
21	315			
22	330			
23	345			
24	360			
	Danger : Severe Shock			
25	375			
26	390			
27	405			
28	420			
	XXX			
29	435			
30	450			
	Mean maximum shock level	8.20	9.35	9.15
	Percentage predicting defiance	100.00%	100.00%	100.00%

* n refers to the number of subjects in the experimental condition.
† These subjects indicated they would refuse to administer even the lowest shock.

of what is desirable and assume that action follows accordingly. But they show little insight into the web of forces that operate in a real social situation.

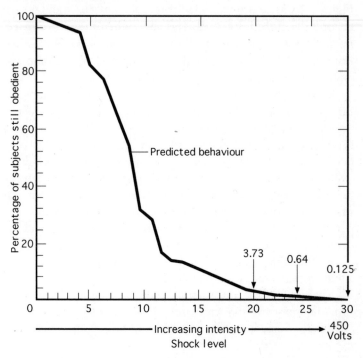

Fig. 5 Psychiatrists' prediction of behaviour in Voice-Feedback Experiment

Perhaps the question posed to them was unfair. People like to see themselves in a favourable light. So we asked also a somewhat different question to eliminate the bias induced by vanity. We asked them to predict how other people would perform. (And more specifically, we requested that they plot the distribution of breakoff points of one hundred Americans of diverse ages and occupations.) Psychiatrists, graduate students and faculty in the behavioural sciences, college sophomores, and middle-class adults responded to the question, and there is remarkable similarity in the predictions of the several groups. They predict that virtually all subjects will refuse to obey the experimenter; only a pathological fringe, not exceeding one or two percent, was expected to proceed to the end of the shockboard. The psychiatrists' predictions are shown in detail in Figure 5 (p. 31). They predicted that most subjects would not go beyond the 10th shock level (150 volts, when the victim makes his first explicit demand to be freed); about 4 percent would reach the 20th shock level, and about one subject in a thousand would administer the highest shock on the board.

What are the assumptions that underlie these predictions? First, that people are by and large decent and do not readily hurt the innocent. Second, that unless coerced by physical force or threat, the individual is preeminently the source of his own behaviour. A person acts in a particular way because he has decided to do so. Action takes place in a physical-social setting, but this is merely the stage for its occurrence. The behaviour itself flows from an inner core of the person; within the core personal values are weighed, gratifications assessed, and resulting decisions are translated into action.

Most people start with presuppositions of this sort when asked to think about the obedience experiment. They focus on the character of the autonomous individual rather than on the situation in which he finds himself. With this view, they are likely to expect few subjects to go along with the experimenter's orders.

CHAPTER 4

CLOSENESS OF THE VICTIM

Now let us look at the actual performance of subjects in the experiment. To begin, we shall consider the results of the Remote-Feedback variation (Experiment 1). It differs slightly from the usual situation in that no vocal complaint is heard from the victim. He is placed in another room where he cannot be seen by the subject, nor can his voice be heard; his answers flash silently on the signal box. However, at 300 volts the laboratory walls resound as he pounds in protest. After 315 volts, no further answers appear, and the pounding ceases.

It is instructive to reprint the subjects' remarks at the point of defiance, as transcribed from the tape recordings:

'I think he's trying to communicate, he's knocking.... Well it's not fair to shock the guy ... these are terrific volts. I don't think this is very humane ... Oh, I can't go on with this; no, this isn't right. It's a hell of an experiment. The guy is suffering in there. No, I don't want to go on. This is crazy.' [Subject refuses to administer more shocks.]

'He's banging in there. I'm gonna chicken out. I'd like to continue, but I can't do that to a man.... I'm sorry I can't do that to a man. I'll hurt his heart. You take your cheque.... No really, I couldn't do it.'

Of the 40 subjects, 26 obeyed the orders of the experimenter to the end, proceeding to punish the victim until they reached the most potent shock available on the generator. After the 450-volt shock was administered three times, the experimenter called a halt to the session.

Subjects were frequently in an agitated state. Sometimes, verbal protest was at a minimum, and the subject simply got up from his chair in front of the shock generator, indicating that he wished to leave the laboratory. Some obedient subjects expressed reluctance to administer shocks beyond the 300-volt level and displayed tensions similar to those who defied the experimenter.

After the maximum shocks had been delivered, and the experimenter called a halt to the proceedings, many obedient subjects heaved sighs of relief, mopped their brows, rubbed their fingers over their eyes, or nervously fumbled cigarettes. Some shook their heads, apparently in regret. Some subjects had remained calm throughout the experiment and displayed only minimal signs of tension from beginning to end.

Bringing the Victim Closer

An experiment differs from a demonstration in that in an experiment, once an effect has been observed, it becomes possible to alter systematically the conditions under which it is produced, and in this way to learn the relevant causes.

What we have seen thus far applies only to a situation in which the victim is out of sight and unable to communicate with his own voice. The recipient of the punishment is thus remote, nor does he indicate his wishes very clearly. There is pounding on the wall, but this has an inherently ambiguous meaning; possibly, some subjects did not interpret this pounding as evidence of the victim's distress. The resulting obedience may be attributable to this. Perhaps there will be no obedience when the victim's suffering is more clearly communicated; when the victim is given a sense of presence, and he is seen, heard, and felt.

Behaviour noted in our pilot studies lent credence to this notion. In those studies the victim could be dimly perceived by the subject through a silvered glass. Subjects frequently averted their eyes from the person they were shocking, often turning their heads in an awkward and conspicuous manner. One subject explained, 'I didn't want to see the consequences of what I had done.' Observers noted:

. . . subjects show a reluctance to look at the victim, whom they could see through the glass in front of them. When this fact was brought to their attention, they indicated that it caused them discomfort to see the victim in agony. We note, however, that although the subject refuses to look at the victim, he continues to administer shocks.

This suggested that the salience of the victim may have, in some degree, regulated the subject's performance. If in obeying the experimenter the subject found it necessary to avoid scrutiny of the victim, would the reverse be true? If the victim were rendered increasingly more salient to the subject, would obedience diminish? A set of four experiments was designed to answer this question. We have already described the Remote condition.

Experiment 2 (Voice-Feedback) was identical to the first except that vocal protests were introduced. As in the first condition, the victim was placed in an adjacent room, but his complaints could be heard clearly through the walls of the laboratory.

Experiment 3 (Proximity) was similar to the second, except that the victim was placed in the same room as the subject, a few feet from him. Thus he was visible as well as audible, and voice cues were provided.

Experiment 4 (Touch-Proximity) was identical to the third, with this exception: the victim received a shock only when his hand rested on a shock plate. At the 150-volt level the victim demanded to be let free and refused to place his hand on the shock plate. The experimenter ordered the subject to force the victim's hand onto the plate. Thus obedience in this condition required that the subject have physical contact with the victim in order to give him punishment at or beyond the 150-volt level.

Forty adult subjects were studied in each condition. The results, shown in Table 2, revealed that obedience was significantly reduced as the victim was rendered more immediate to the subject. The mean maximum shock for the conditions is shown in Figure 6.

Table 2. Maximum Shocks Administered in Experiments 1, 2, 3, and 4

Shock level	Verbal designation and voltage level	Experiment 1 Remote (n = 40)	Experiment 2 Voice-Feedback (n = 40)	Experiment 3 Proximity (n = 40)	Experiment 4 Touch-Proximity (n = 40)
	Slight shock				
1	15				
2	30				
3	45				
4	60				
	Moderate Shock				
5	75				
6	90				
7	105			1	
8	120				
	Strong Shock				
9	135		1		1
10	150		5	10	16
11	165		1		
12	180		1	2	3
	Very Strong Shock				
13	195				
14	210				1
15	225			1	1
16	240				
	Intense Shock				
17	255				1
18	270			1	
19	285		1		1
20	300	5°	1	5	1
	Extreme Intensity Shock				
21	315	4	3	3	2
22	330	2			
23	345	1	1		1
24	360	1	1		
	Danger : Severe Shock				
25	375	1		1	
26	390				
27	405				
28	420				
	XXX				
29	435				
30	450	26	25	16	12
	Mean maximum shock level	27.0	24.53	20.80	17.88
	Percentage obedient subjects	65.0%	62.5%	40.0%	30.0%

° Indicates that in Experiment 1, five subjects administered a maximum shock of 300 volts.

Thirty-five percent of the subjects defied the experimenter in the Remote condition, 37.5 percent in Voice-Feedback, 60 percent in Proximity, and 70 percent in Touch-Proximity.

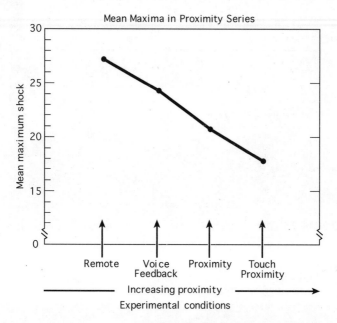

Fig. 6 Mean maximum shocks in Experiments 1, 2, 3 and 4

How are we to account for the diminishing obedience as the victim is brought closer? Several factors may be at work.

1. *Empathic cues.* In the Remote and, to a lesser extent, the Voice-Feedback conditions, the victim's suffering possesses an abstract, remote quality for the subject. He is aware, but only in a conceptual sense, that his actions cause pain to another person; the fact is apprehended but not felt. The phenomenon is common enough. The bombardier can reasonably suppose that his weapons will inflict suffering and death, yet this knowledge is divested of affect and does not arouse in him an emotional response to the suffering he causes.

It is possible that the visual cues associated with the victim's suffering trigger empathic responses in the subject and give him

General arrangement for Touch-Proximity Condition

Fig. 7

Obedient subject in Touch-Proximity Condition

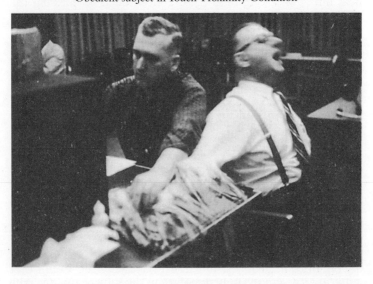

a more complete grasp of the victim's experience. It is also possible that the empathic responses are themselves unpleasant, possessing drive properties which cause the subject to terminate the arousal situation. Diminishing obedience, then, would be explained by the enrichment of empathic cues in the successive experimental conditions.

2. *Denial and narrowing of the cognitive field*. The Remote condition allows a narrowing of the cognitive field so that the victim is put out of mind. When the victim is close it is more difficult to exclude him from thought. He necessarily intrudes on the subject's awareness, since he is continuously visible. In the first two conditions his existence and reactions are made known only after the shock has been administered. The auditory feedback is sporadic and discontinuous. In the Proximity conditions his inclusion in the immediate visual field renders him a continuously salient element for the subject. The mechanism of denial can no longer be brought into play. One subject in the Remote condition said, 'It's funny how you really begin to forget that there's a guy out there, even though you can hear him. For a long time I just concentrated on pressing the switches and reading the words.'

3. *Reciprocal fields*. If, in the Proximity conditions, the subject is in an improved position to observe the victim, the reverse is also true: the actions of the subject now come under scrutiny by the victim. Possibly, it is easier to harm a person when he is unable to observe our actions than when he can see what we are doing. His surveillance of the action directed against him may give rise to shame or guilt, which may then serve to curtail the action. Many expressions of language refer to the discomfort or inhibitions that arise in face-to-face attack. It is often said that it is easier to criticise a man 'behind his back' than to confront him directly. If we are lying to someone, it is reputedly difficult to 'look him in the eye'. We 'turn away in shame' or in 'embarrassment', and this action serves to reduce our discomfort. The manifest function of allowing the victim of a firing squad to be blindfolded is to make the occasion less

stressful for him, but it may also serve a latent function of reducing the stress of the executioner. In short, in the Proximity conditions, the subject may sense that he has become more salient in the victim's field of awareness and consequently becomes more self-conscious, embarrassed, and inhibited in his punishment of the victim.

4. *Experienced unity of act.* In the Remote conditions it is more difficult for the subject to see a connection between his actions and their consequences for the victim. There is a physical separation of the act and its effects. The subject depresses a lever in one room, and protests and cries are heard from another. The two events are in correlation, yet they lack a compelling unity. The unity is more fully achieved in the Proximity conditions as the victim is brought closer to the action that causes him pain. It is rendered complete in Touch-Proximity.

5. *Incipient group-formation.* Placing the victim in another room not only takes him farther from the subject, it also draws the subject and the experimenter relatively closer. There is incipient group formation between the experimenter and the subject, from which the victim is excluded. The wall between the victim and the others deprives him of an intimacy which the experimenter and the subject could feel. In the Remote condition, the victim is truly an outsider, who stands alone, physically and psychologically.

When the victim is placed close to the subject, it becomes easier to form an alliance with him against the experimenter. The subject no longer has to face the experimenter alone. He has an ally who is close at hand and eager to collaborate in a revolt against the experimenter. Thus, the changing set of spatial relations leads to a potentially shifting set of alliances over the several experimental conditions.

6. *Acquired behaviour dispositions.* It is commonly observed that laboratory mice will rarely fight with their litter mates. Scott (1958) explains this in terms of passive inhibition. He writes: 'By doing nothing under ... circumstances [the animal] learns to do

nothing, and this may be spoken of as passive inhibition. . . . This principle has great importance in teaching an individual to be peaceful, for it means that he can learn not to fight simply by not fighting.' Similarly, we may learn not to harm others simply by not harming them in everyday life. Yet this learning occurs in a context of proximal relations with others and may not be generalised to situations in which the others are physically remote from us. Or perhaps, in the past, aggressive actions against others who were physically close resulted in retaliatory punishment that extinguished the original form of response. In contrast, aggression against others at a distance may rarely have led to retaliation.

We move about; our spatial relations shift from one situation to the next, and the fact that we are near or remote may have a powerful effect on the psychological processes that mediate our behaviour toward others. In these experiments, as the victim was brought closer to the man ordered to give him shocks, increasing numbers of subjects broke off the experiment, refusing to obey. The concrete, visible, and proximal presence of the victim acted in an important way to counteract the experimenter's power and to generate disobedience. Any theoretical model of obedience will have to take this fact into account.

Unexpected Behaviour

The overall level of obedience, across all four experimental variations, requires comment. Subjects have learned from childhood that it is a fundamental breach of moral conduct to hurt another person against his will. Yet, almost half the subjects abandon this tenet in following the instructions of an authority who has no special powers to enforce his commands. To disobey would bring no material loss or punishment. It is clear from the remarks and behaviour of many participants that in punishing the victim they were often acting against their own values. Subjects often expressed disapproval of shocking a man in the face of his objections, and others denounced it as stupid and

senseless. Yet many followed the experimental commands.

The results differed sharply from the predictions made in the questionnaire described earlier. (Here, however, it is possible that the remoteness of the respondents from the actual situation and the difficulty of conveying to them the concrete details of the experiment could account for the serious underestimation of obedience.) But the results were also unexpected to people who observed the experiment in progress through one-way mirrors. Observers often expressed disbelief upon seeing a subject administer more and more powerful shocks to the victim; even persons fully acquainted with the details of the situation consistently underestimated the amount of obedience subjects would display.

The second unanticipated effect was the tension generated by the procedures. One might suppose that a subject would simply break off or continue as his conscience dictated. This is very far from what happened. There were in some subjects striking reactions of emotional strain.

In the interview following the experiment subjects were asked to indicate on a 14-point scale just how nervous or tense

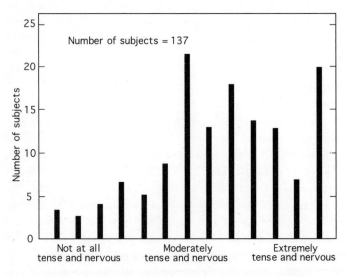

Fig. 8 Level of tension and nervousness reported by subjects

they felt at the point of maximum tension (Figure 8). The scale ranged from 'Not at all tense and nervous' to 'Extremely tense and nervous'. Self-reports of this sort are of limited precision and at best provide only a rough indication of the subject's emotional response. Still, taking the reports for what they are worth, it can be seen that the distribution of responses spans the entire range of the scale, with the majority of subjects concentrated at the centre and upper extreme. A further breakdown showed that obedient subjects reported themselves as having been slightly more tense and nervous than the defiant subjects at the point of maximum tension.

How is the occurrence of tension to be interpreted? First, it points to the presence of conflict. If a tendency to comply with authority were the only psychological force operating in the situation, all subjects would have continued to the end, and there would have been no tension. Tension, it is assumed, results from the simultaneous presence of two or more incompatible response tendencies (Miller, 1944). If sympathetic concern for the victim were the exclusive force, all subjects would have calmly defied the experimenter. Instead, there were both obedient and defiant outcomes, frequently accompanied by extreme tension. A conflict develops between the deeply ingrained disposition not to harm others and the equally compelling tendency to obey others who are in authority. The subject is quickly drawn into a dilemma, and the presence of high tension points to the considerable strength of each of the antagonistic vectors.

Moreover, tension defines the strength of the aversive state from which the subject is unable to escape through disobedience. When a person is uncomfortable, tense, or stressed, he tries to take some action that will allow him to terminate this unpleasant state. Thus tension may serve as a drive that leads to escape behaviour. But in the present situation even where tension is extreme, many subjects are unable to perform the response that will bring about relief. Therefore there must be a competing drive, tendency, or inhibition that precludes activation of the disobedient response. The strength of this inhibiting factor must be of greater magnitude than the stress

experienced, or else the terminating act would occur. Every evidence of extreme tension is at the same time an indication of the strength of the forces that keep the subject in the situation.

Finally, tension may be taken as evidence of the reality of the situation for the subject. Normal subjects do not tremble and sweat unless they are implicated in a deep and genuinely felt predicament.

CHAPTER 5

INDIVIDUALS CONFRONT AUTHORITY

From each person in the experiment we derive one essential fact: whether he has obeyed or disobeyed. But it is foolish to see the subject only in this way. For he brings to the laboratory a full range of emotions, attitudes, and individual styles. Indeed, so varied in temperament and manner are the people passing through the laboratory that it sometimes seems a miracle that we emerge with any regularities at all. One subject may be an inarticulate bricklayer, diffident and awkwardly humble in the presence of a scientist. He is followed by a self-assured businessman, who thrusts his cigar at the experimenter to underscore his assertions.

We need to focus on the individuals who took part in the study not only because this provides a personal dimension to the experiment but also because the quality of each person's experience gives us clues to the nature of the process of obedience.

We shall rely heavily on the participant's own comments and assertions in building up the picture. At the same time a warning is in order. While we must take very seriously everything the subject says, we need not necessarily think that he fully understands the causes of his own behaviour. A line must be drawn between listening carefully to what the subject says and mistaking it for the full story. The subject is controlled by many forces in the situation beyond his awareness, implicit structures that regulate his behaviour without signalling this fact to him. And we have one enormous advantage over the subject: In each condition, we have slightly varied the nature of the circumstances which the subject confronts and thus know the importance of each of the factors. The participant, and he alone, has experienced the predicament, but he cannot place it in the perspective that comes only from an overview.

The sources of information are, first, our observation of the individual as he performs in the experiment – in particular, the dialogue arising between him and the experimenter. Additionally, all subjects provided information on their background in a post-experimental interview (we have changed their names in the following accounts). Finally, a number of subjects took part in individual and group discussions, led by a member of the Yale School of Psychiatry.

Bruno Batta, Welder (in Experiment 4)

Mr Batta is a thirty-seven-year-old welder. He was born in New Haven, his parents in Italy. He has a rough-hewn face that conveys a conspicuous lack of alertness. His over-all appearance is somewhat brutish. An observer described him as a 'crude mesomorph of obviously limited intelligence.' But this is not fully adequate, for he relates to the experimenter with a submissive and deferential sweetness.

He has some difficulty in mastering the experimental procedure and needs to be corrected by the experimenter several times. He shows appreciation for the help and willingness to do what is required. The experiment is the Touch-Proximity variation. After the 150-volt level, Batta has to force the learner's hand down on the shock plate, since the learner himself refuses to touch it.

When the learner first complains, Mr Batta pays no attention to him. His face remains impassive, as if to dissociate himself from the learner's disruptive behaviour. When the experimenter instructs him to force the learner's hand down, he adopts a rigid mechanical procedure. He tests the generator switch. When it fails to function, he immediately forces the learner's hand onto the shock plate. All the while he maintains the same rigid mask. The learner, seated alongside him, begs him to stop, but with robotic impassivity, he continues the procedure. What is extraordinary is his apparent total indifference to the learner; he hardly takes cognisance of him as a human being. Meanwhile, he relates to the experimenter in a submissive and courteous fashion.

At the 330-volt level, the learner refuses not only to touch the shock plate but also to provide any answers. Annoyed, Batta turns to him, and chastises him: 'You better answer and get it over with. We can't stay here all night.' These are the only words he directs to the learner in the course of the hour. Never again does he speak to him. The scene is brutal and depressing: his hard, impassive face showing total indifference as he subdues the screaming learner and gives him shocks. He seems to derive no pleasure from the act itself, only quiet satisfaction at doing his job properly.

When he administers 450 volts, he turns to the experimenter and asks, 'Where do we go from here, Professor?' His tone is deferential and expresses his willingness to be a cooperative subject, in contrast to the learner's obstinacy.

In the postexperimental interview, he gives a jumbled account of the experiment. The experimenter routinely asks him whether the experiment has any other purpose he can think of. He uses the question, without any particular logic, to denigrate the learner, stating, 'Well, we have more or less a stubborn person (the learner). If he understood what this here was, he would'a went along without getting the punishment.' In his view, the learner brought punishment on himself.

The experimenter asks whether he felt tense or nervous during the experiment. Again, he uses the question to express his feelings toward the learner. 'The only time I got a little – I wouldn't say nervous – I got *disgusted*, is when he wouldn't cooperate.' The experimenter has great difficulty in questioning the subject on the issue of responsibility. He does not seem to grasp the concept. The interviewer simplifies the question. Finally the subject assigns major responsibility to the experimenter: 'I say your fault for the simple reason that I was paid for doing this. I had to follow orders. That's how I figured it.'

Then, assigning all possibilities of initiative to the experimenter, he says, 'Now you could have just as soon said, "Now look, gimme the money back and we'll forget about this thing." Then we could have made up our own minds.'

We note that while for many subjects offering to return the

payment is regarded as an honourable means of withdrawing from the experiment, this subject can only conceive of the act if initiated by the authority. The experimenter rejoins, 'But I told you the money was yours simply for coming, no matter what happened.'

'That's right.'

At the end of the session, he tells the experimenter how honoured he has been to help him, and in a moment of contrition, remarks, 'Sir, sorry it couldn't have been a full experiment.'

He has done his honest best. It is only the deficient behaviour of the learner that has denied the experimenter full satisfaction.

In a questionnaire returned by Mr Batta several months later, he informs us that he followed the experimenter's instructions to the end, that he fully believed the learner was getting painful shocks, and that the experiment has not bothered him at all. He believes more experiments of this sort should be carried out, and he answers 'yes' to our question of whether he has learned something of personal value. But he does not tell us what.

Professor of Old Testament (in Experiment 3)

A somewhat gaunt, ascetic man, this subject could be taken for a New England minister. In fact, he teaches Old Testament liturgy at a major divinity school. In this Proximity condition, he adjusted his seat to look at the learner while administering shocks. While reading the word pairs, he employs exaggerated precision in his pronunciation, and seems curt and officious in saying, 'Correct.' Whenever the learner makes an error, he appears almost to be chastising him for his failing. Each time he administers a shock, his lips are drawn back, and he bares his teeth. An excessive fastidiousness characterises all his actions. After administering 150 volts he balks at going further. The experimenter states that the learner's protests are to be disregarded, and the experiment must continue:

EXPERIMENTER: It's absolutely essential to the experiment that we continue.

SUBJECT: I understand that statement, but I don't understand why the experiment is placed above this person's life.

EXPERIMENTER: There is no permanent tissue damage.

SUBJECT: Well, that's your opinion. If he doesn't want to continue, I'm taking orders from him.

EXPERIMENTER: You have no other choice, sir, you must go on.

SUBJECT: If this were Russia maybe, but not in America.

[The experiment is terminated.]

In his discussion with the experimenter, the subject seems in no way intimidated by the experimenter's status but rather treats him as a dull technician who does not see the full implications of what he is doing. When the experimenter assures him of the safety of the shock generator, the subject, with some exasperation, brings up the question of the emotional rather than physiological effects on the learner.

SUBJECT: [spontaneously]: Surely you've considered the ethics of this thing. [extremely agitated] Here he doesn't want to go on, and you think that the experiment is more important? Have you examined him? Do you know what his physical state is? Say this man had a weak heart [quivering voice].

EXPERIMENTER: We know the machine, sir.

SUBJECT: But you don't know the man you're experimenting on. . . . That's very risky [gulping and tremulous]. What about the fear that man had? It's impossible for you to determine what effect that has on him. . . . the fear that he himself is generating. . . . But go ahead, you ask me questions; I'm not here to question you.

He limits his questioning, first because he asserts he does not have a right to question, but one feels that he considers the experimenter too rigid and limited a technician to engage in intelligent dialogue. One notes further his spontaneous mention of *ethics*, raised in a didactic manner and deriving from his professional position as teacher of religion. Finally, it is

49

interesting that he initially justified his breaking off the experiment not by asserting disobedience but by asserting that he would then take orders from the victim.

Thus, he speaks of an equivalence between the experimenter's and the learner's orders and does not disobey so much as shifts the person from whom he will take orders.

After explaining the true purpose of the experiment, the experimenter asks, 'What in your opinion is the most effective way of strengthening resistance to inhumane authority?'

The subject answers, 'If one had as one's ultimate authority God, then it trivialises human authority.'

Again, the answer for this man lies not in the repudiation of authority but in the substitution of good – that is, divine – authority for bad.

Jack Washington, Drill Press Operator (in Experiment 2)

Jack Washington is a black subject, age thirty-five, who was born in South Carolina. He works as a drill press operator and stresses the fact that although he did not complete high school, he was not a dropout but was drafted into the army before he could get his diploma. He is a soft man, a bit heavy and balding, older-looking than his years. His pace is very slow and his manner impassive; his speech is tinged with Southern and black accents.

When the victim's first protests are heard, he turns toward the experimenter, looks sadly at him, then continues reading the word pairs. The experimenter does not have to tell him to continue. Throughout the experiment he shows almost no emotion or bodily movement. He does what the experimenter tells him in a slow, steady pace that is set off sharply against the strident cries of the victim. Throughout, a sad, dejected expression shows on his face. He continues to the 450-volt level, asks the experimenter what he is to do at that point, administers two additional shocks on command, and is relieved of his task.

He explains in the interview that although he feels the shocks were extremely painful, he accepted the experimenter's word that they would cause no permanent damage. He reaffirms this belief in a questionnaire answered almost a year after his participation. When asked about responsibility for the victim's suffering, he places the heaviest burden on the experimenter, then on the victim, and assigns the least to himself. Of the learner he says, 'He agreed to it, and therefore must accept responsibility.' The experimenter has 'the biggest share of the responsibility. I merely went on. Because I was following orders . . . I was told to go on. And I did not get a cue to stop.'

He becomes enmeshed in this formulation, which he repeats several times. He explains to the experimenter that if he had received a cue from the experimenter, he would have stopped, implying that he would behave in whatever manner the experimenter required. The only dereliction he can conceive of in the situation is that of not obeying the experimenter.

He explains in his slow, steady manner, 'I know that up to a certain point a shock won't kill you. I had a shock to the point where I was almost knocked down. . . . My whole hand was numb. But it didn't kill me.'

Thus, he indicates acceptance of the experimenter's statement that the shocks may be painful but are not dangerous. In all respects he expresses total faith in the experimenter and indeed accepts his authority more easily and with less inner conflict than many subjects.

Jan Rensaleer, Industrial Engineer (in Experiment 2)

The subject is a thirty-two-year-old industrial engineer, sporting blond hair and a moustache. He is self-contained and speaks with a trace of a foreign accent. He is neatly dressed. In the interview he tells us that he emigrated from Holland after the Second World War and that he is a member of the Dutch Reformed Church. He is mild-mannered and intelligent.

When the victim complains at the 150-volt level, the subject turns to the experimenter and asks, 'What do I do now?'

The experimenter tells him to continue.

The engineer presses his hand to his head and proceeds with

the test. He glances more and more often at the experimenter. At 255 volts, he pushes the chair away from the shock generator and turns to the experimenter:

MR RENSALEER: Oh, I can't continue this way; it's a voluntary program, if the man doesn't want to go on with it.

EXPERIMENTER: Please continue.

[A long pause.]

MR RENSALEER: No, I can't continue. I'm sorry.

EXPERIMENTER: The experiment requires that you go on.

MR RENSALEER: The man, he seems to be getting hurt.

EXPERIMENTER: There is no permanent tissue damage.

MR RENSALEER: Yes, but I know what shocks do to you. I'm an electrical engineer, and I have had shocks . . . and you get real shook up by them − especially if you know the next one is coming. I'm sorry.

EXPERIMENTER: It is absolutely essential that you continue.

MR RENSALEER: Well, I won't − not with the man screaming to get out.

EXPERIMENTER: You have no other choice.

MR RENSALEER: I do have a choice. [Incredulous and indignant:] Why don't I have a choice? I came here on my own free will. I thought I could help in a research project. But if I have to hurt somebody to do that, or if I was in his place, too, I wouldn't stay there. I can't continue. I'm very sorry. I think I've gone too far already, probably.

When asked who was responsible for shocking the learner against his will, he said, 'I would put it on myself entirely.'

He refused to assign any responsibility to the learner or the experimenter.

'I should have stopped the first time he complained. I did want to stop at that time. I turned around and looked at you. I guess it's a matter of . . . authority, if you want to call it that: my being impressed by the thing, and going on although I didn't want to. Say, if you're serving in the army, and you have to do something you don't like to do, but your superior tells you to do it. That sort of thing, you know what I mean?

'One of the things I think is very cowardly is to try to shove the responsibility onto someone else. See, if I now turned around and said, "It's your fault . . . it's not mine," I would call that cowardly.'

Although this subject defied the experimenter at 255 volts, he still feels responsible for administering any shocks beyond the victim's first protests. He is hard on himself and does not allow the structure of authority in which he is functioning to absolve him of any responsibility.

Mr Rensaleer expressed surprise at the underestimation of obedience by the psychiatrists. He said that on the basis of his experience in Nazi-occupied Europe, he would predict a high level of compliance to orders. He suggests, 'It would be interesting to conduct the same tests in Germany and other countries.'[3]

The experiment made a deep impression on the subject, so much so that a few days after his participation he wrote a long, careful letter to the staff, asking if he could work with us.

'Although I am . . . employed in engineering, I have become convinced that the social sciences and especially psychology, are much more important in today's world.'

Morris Braverman, Social Worker (in Experiment 2)

Morris Braverman is a thirty-nine-year-old social worker. He looks older than his years because of his bald pate and serious demeanour. His brow is furrowed, as if all the world's burdens were carried in his face. He appears intelligent and concerned. The impression he creates is that of enormous overcontrol, that of a repressed and serious man, whose finely modulated voice is not linked with his emotional life. He speaks impressively but with perceptible affectation. As the experiment proceeds, laughter intrudes into his performance. At first, it is a light snicker, then it becomes increasingly insistent and disruptive. The laughter seemed triggered by the learner's screams.

When the learner refuses to answer and the experimenter instructs him to treat the absence of an answer as equivalent to a wrong answer, he takes his instruction to heart.

Before administering 315 volts he asserts officiously to the victim, 'Mr Wallace, your silence has to be considered as a wrong answer.' Then he administers the shock. He offers half-heartedly to change places with the learner, then asks the experimenter, 'Do I have to follow these instructions literally?' He is satisfied with the experimenter's answer that he does. His very refined and authoritative manner of speaking is increasingly broken up by wheezing laughter.

The experimenter's notes on Mr Braverman at the last few shocks are:

> Almost breaking up now each time gives shock. Rubbing face to hide laughter.
> Ratting eyes, trying to hide face with hand, still laughing.
> Cannot control his laughter at this point no matter what he does.
> Clenching fist, pushing it onto table.

In the interview, Mr Braverman summarises the experiment with impressive fluency and intelligence. He feels the experiment may have been designed also to 'test the effects on the teacher of being in an essentially sadistic role, as well as the reactions of a student to a learning situation that was authoritative, rigid, and punitive.' When asked how painful the last few shocks administered to the learner were, he indicates that the most extreme category on the scale is not adequate (it read EXTREMELY PAINFUL) and places his mark at the extreme edge of the scale with an arrow carrying it beyond the scale.

It is almost impossible to convey the extremely relaxed, sedate quality of his conversation in the interview. In the most quiescent terms, he speaks about his extreme inner tension.

EXPERIMENTER: At what point were you most tense or nervous?

MR BRAVERMAN: Well, when he first began to cry in pain, and I realised this was hurting him. This got worse when he just blocked and refused to answer. There was I. I'm a nice person, I think, hurting somebody, and caught up in what seemed a mad situation . . . and in the interest of science, one goes through with it. At one point I had an impulse to just refuse to continue with this kind of a teaching situation.

EXPERIMENTER: At what point was this?

MR BRAVERMAN: This was after a couple of successive refusals and silences. This is when I asked you a question as to whether I have a choice in my teaching method. At this point my impulse was to plead with him, talk with him, encourage him, try to ally myself with his feelings, work at this so we could get this through together and I wouldn't have to hurt him.

When Mr Braverman states that he considered 'not going through with it', he does not mean that he considered disobeying but rather that he considered modifying the manner of teaching the victim.

When the interviewer brings up the general question of tension, Mr Braverman spontaneously mentions his laughter.

'My reactions were awfully peculiar. I don't know if you were watching me, but my reactions were giggly, and trying to stifle laughter. This isn't the way I usually am. This was a sheer reaction to a totally impossible situation. And my reaction was to the situation of having to hurt somebody. And being totally helpless and caught up in a set of circumstances where I just couldn't deviate and I couldn't try to help. This is what got me.'

A year after his participation in the experiment, he affirms in the questionnaire that he has definitely learned something of personal importance as a result of being in the experiment, adding: 'What appalled me was that I could possess this capacity for obedience and compliance to a central idea, i.e. the value of a memory experiment even after it became clear that continued adherence to this value was at the expense of violation of another value, i.e don't hurt someone else who is helpless and not hurting you. As my wife said, "You can call yourself Eichmann." I hope I can deal more effectively with any future conflicts of values I encounter.'

CHAPTER 6

FURTHER VARIATIONS AND CONTROLS

Experiment 5: A New Base-Line Condition

After the proximity series was completed, the experiment was moved out of the elegant Yale Interaction Laboratory to more modest quarters in the basement of the same building. The new laboratory was functional but somewhat plain, with bare steam pipes running along the ceiling, and a concrete floor, instead of the posh rugs and drapes of the former locale. I wondered whether the less impressive quarters would lead to a lesser level of obedience. In any case it was necessary to establish a new base-line condition. It was modelled on the Voice-Feedback condition, with a slight alteration. The learner would not merely respond with cries of anguish, but would introduce remarks about a heart problem. Perhaps this new element would provide additional justification for disobeying and make such a course of action seem even more compelling and necessary.

I did not wish to make the 'heart problem' so serious that it would disqualify the learner from participation but merely to raise a suggestion of a problem. This was achieved through remarks made by the victim at the time he was being strapped into the electric chair. The experimenter and naïve subject (who has assisted strapping the learner into the chair) are about to leave the learner and return to the control room. The experimenter routinely asks, 'Any questions?' The learner responds somewhat diffidently, 'When I was at the Westhaven V.A. Hospital, a few years ago, they detected a slight heart condition. Nothing serious, but are these shocks dangerous?'

The experimenter replies in a confident, somewhat dismissive tone that although the shocks may be painful, they cause no permanent tissue damage, and then proceeds with the experimental routines.

The new series of protests, which was to serve as a standard for all subsequent experiments, paralleled the first set, with the exception that reference is made to the learner's heart condition at 150, 195, and 330 volts. The exact schedule of protests is as follows:

Experiment 5: New Base-Line Condition
The Learner's Schedule of Protests

75 volts   Ugh!

90 volts   Ugh!

105 volts   Ugh! [louder]

120 volts   Ugh! Hey, this really hurts.

135 volts   Ugh!!

150 volts   Ugh!!! Experimenter! That's all. Get me out of here. I told you I had heart trouble. My heart's starting to bother me now. Get me out of here, please. My heart's starting to bother me. I refuse to go on. Let me out.

165 volts   Ugh! Let me out! [shouting]

180 volts   Ugh! I can't stand the pain. Let me out of here! [shouting]

195 volts   Ugh! Let me out of here. Let me out of here. My heart's bothering me. Let me out of here! You have no right to keep me here! Let me out! Let me out of here! Let me out! Let me out of here! My heart's bothering me. Let me out! Let me out!

210 volts   Ugh!! Experimenter! Get me out of here. I've had enough. I won't be in the experiment any more.

225 volts   Ugh!

240 volts   Ugh!

255 volts   Ugh! Get me out of here.

270 volts   [Agonised scream.] Let me out of here. Let me out of here. Let me out of here. Let me out. Do you hear? Let me out of here.

285 volts   [Agonised scream.]

300 volts   [Agonised scream.] I absolutely refuse to answer any more. Get me out of here. You can't hold me here. Get me out. Get me out of here.

315 volts   [Intensely agonised scream.] I told you I refuse to answer. I'm no longer part of this experiment.

330 volts   [Intense and prolonged agonised scream.] Let me out of here. Let me out of here. My heart's bothering me. Let me out, I tell you. [Hysterically.] Let me out of here. Let me out of here. You have no right to hold me here. Let me out! Let me out! Let me out! Let me out of here! Let me out! Let me out!

Neither the less elegant laboratory nor the mention of a heart condition leads to greater disobedience. Twenty-six of the 40 subjects continued to the end in the present condition, compared with 25 out of 40 in the Voice-Feedback condition, merely a slight chance variation. The distribution of breakoff points is shown in Table 3.

Probably there is nothing the victim can say that will uniformly generate disobedience; for the teacher's actions are not controlled by him.

In the postexperimental interview subjects were asked, 'What is the maximum sample shock you would be willing to accept?' The data are available for 39 subjects in this condition and are shown in Figure 9. Three defiant subjects would accept shocks more powerful than they had administered. Of the 26 obedient subjects, 7 were willing to sample the 450-volt shock they had just administered, while 19 were not. In most cases there is a marked discrepancy between the shock the subject administered and the level he would be willing to accept as a sample. Thus three lowest dots in the extreme right side of the graph represent three subjects who administered 450 volts but would not be willing to sample more than 45 volts. Similar and even more extreme results are found in all experimental conditions when this question was asked.

Experiment 6: Change of Personnel

Is it possible that the subjects respond principally to the personalities of the experimenter and victim? Perhaps the experimenter came across as a more forceful person than the

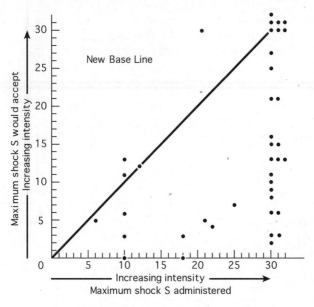

Fig. 9 Maximum shock subject would
accept as a function of shock administered

victim, and the subject allied himself with the more impressive
personality. The following experimental comparison came
about inadvertently, but it can shed some light on this point. In
order to speed up the running of the experiment, we had set up
a second team, consisting of a new experimenter and a new
victim. In the first team the experimenter was a somewhat dry,
hard, technical looking man. The victim in contrast was soft,
avuncular, and innocuous. These personal characteristics were
more or less reversed in the second team. The new
experimenter was rather soft and unaggressive. The alternate
victim, in contrast, was played by a man possessing a hard bony
face and prognothic jaw, who looked as if he would do well in
a scrap. The results, shown in Table 3, indicate that the change
in personnel had little effect on the level of obedience. The
personal characteristics of the experimenter and victim were
not of overriding importance.

Table 3. Maximum Shocks Administered in Experiments 5-11.

Shock level	Verbal designation and voltage level	Experiment 5: New Base line (n = 40)	Experiment 6: Change of Personnel (n = 40)	Experiment 7: Experimenter Absent (n = 40)
	Slight shock			
1	15			
2	30			
3	45			
4	60			
	Moderate Shock			
5	75			
6	90	1		1
7	105			1
8	120		2	
	Strong Shock			
9	135			1
10	150	6	4	7
11	165		1	3
12	180	1	3	1
	Very Strong Shock			
13	195		1	5
14	210		2	
15	225			1
16	240			
	Intense Shock			
17	255			
18	270	2	2	3
19	285			
20	300	1	1	3
	Extreme Intensity Shock			
21	315	1	2	
22	330	1	1	1
23	345			
24	360		1	2
	Danger : Severe Shock			
25	375	1		
26	390			
27	405			
28	420			1
	XXX			1
29	435			
30	450	26	20	9
	Mean maximum shock level	24.55	22.20	18.15
	Percentage administering maximum shock	65.0%	50.0%	20.5%

Table 3. (contd.)

Shock level	Verbal designation and voltage level	Experiment 8: Women (n = 40)	Experiment 9: Enters with Prior Conditions (n = 40)	Experiment 10: Office Building, Bridgport (n = 40)	Experiment 11: Subject Chooses Shock Level‡ (n = 40)
	Slight shock			2*	
1	15				3
2	30				6
3	45				7
4	60				7
	Moderate Shock				
5	75				5
6	90			1	4
7	105				1
8	120				1
	Strong Shock				
9	135		1		3
10	150	4	7	7	1
11	165	1	2		
12	180	2	1	1	
	Very Strong Shock				
13	195		1	3	
14	210	1			
15	225				
16	240		1		
	Intense Shock				
17	255		1	1	
18	270	2	2		
19	285				
20	300	1	1	4	
	Extreme Intensity Shock				
21	315	2	3	1	
22	330			1	
23	345		1		
24	360		1		
	Danger : Severe Shock				
25	375		1		1
26	390		1		
27	405				
28	420				
	XXX				
29	435				
30	450	26	16	19	1
	Mean maximum shock level	24.73	21.40	20.95	5.50
	Percentage obedient subjects	65.0%	40.0%	47.5%	2.5%‡

* Two subjects in Bridgport refused to administer even the lowest shock.
† Indicates the maximum shock chosen by the subject, no matter at what point it occurred in his sequence of choices.
‡ Percentage of subjects who used the last shock on the generator. Does not indicate obedience, as subjects chose their own level.

Experiment 7: Closeness of Authority

We saw in the proximity experiments that the spatial relationship between subject and victim affected the level of obedience. Would not the relationship of subject to experimenter also play a part?

There are reasons to feel that, on arrival, the subjects were oriented primarily to the experimenter rather than to the victim. They had come to the laboratory to fit into the structure that the experimenter – not the victim – would provide. They had come less to understand the behaviour than to *reveal* that behaviour to a competent scientist, and they were willing to display themselves as the scientist's purposes required. Most subjects seemed quite concerned about the appearance they were making before the experimenter, and one could argue that this preoccupation in a relatively new and strange setting made the subjects somewhat insensitive to the triadic nature of the social situation. The subjects were so concerned about the show they were putting on for the experimenter that influences from other parts of the social field did not receive much weight. This powerful orientation to the experimenter would account for the relative insensitivity of the subject to the victim and would also lead us to believe that alterations in the relationship between subject and experimenter would have important consequences for obedience.

In another series of experiments we varied the physical closeness of the experimenter and the degree of surveillance he exercised. In Experiment 5 the experimenter sat just a few feet away from the subject. In Experiment 7, after giving initial instructions, the experimenter left the laboratory and gave his orders by telephone.

Obedience dropped sharply when the experimenter was physically removed from the laboratory. The number of obedient subjects in the first condition (26) was almost three times as great as in the second (9), in which the experimenter gave his orders by telephone. Subjects seemed able to resist the experimenter far better when they did not have to confront him face to face.

Moreover, when the experimenter was absent, subjects displayed an interesting form of behaviour that had not occurred under his surveillance. Though continuing with the experiment, several subjects administered lower shocks than were required and never informed the experimenter of their deviation from the correct procedure. Indeed, in telephone conversations some subjects specifically assured the experimenter that they were raising the shock level according to instruction, while, in reality, they repeatedly used the lowest shock on the board. This form of behaviour is particularly interesting: although these subjects acted in a way that clearly undermined the avowed purposes of the experiment, they found it easier to handle the conflict in this manner than to precipitate an open break with authority.

Other conditions were completed in which the experimenter was absent during the first segment of the experiment but reappeared shortly after the subject had refused to give higher shocks when commanded by telephone. Although he had exhausted his power via telephone, the experimenter could frequently force further obedience when he reappeared in the laboratory.

This series of experiments showed that the physical presence of an authority was an important force contributing to the subject's obedience or defiance. Obedience to destructive commands was in some degree dependent on the proximal relations between authority and subject, and any theory of obedience must take account of this fact.[4]

Experiment 8: Women as Subjects

In the experiments described thus far the subjects were adult males. Forty women were also studied. They are of particular theoretical interest because of two general sets of findings in social psychology. First, in most tests of compliance, women are more yielding than men (Weiss, 1969; Feinberg, mimeo). And thus in the present study they might have been expected to show more obedience. On the other hand, women are thought to be less aggressive and more empathic than men; thus their resistance to shocking the victim would also be higher. In principle, the two factors ought to work in opposite directions. The results are shown in Table 3. The level of obedience was virtually identical to the performance of men;[5] however, the level of conflict experienced by the women was on the whole higher than that felt by our male subjects.[6]

There were many specifically feminine styles in handling the conflict. In postexperimental interviews women, far more frequently than men, related their experience to problems of rearing children.

The women were studied only in the role of teachers. It would be interesting to move them into other roles. As victims, they would most likely generate more disobedience, for cultural norms militate against hurting women even more strongly than hurting men. (Similarly, if a child were placed in the victim's role, disobedience would be much greater.)

It would be especially interesting to place women in the position of authority. Here it is unclear how male subjects and other women would respond to her. There is less experience with women bosses; on the other hand many men may want to show their toughness before a woman experimenter, by carrying out her callous orders without emotion. The accounts of three female subjects are given in Chapter 7.

Experiment 9: The Victim's Limited Contract

Some subjects rely on the idea of an implicit social contract in explaining their own obedience. They reasoned thus: they had contracted with the experimenter to relinquish some of their freedom in the pursuit of a commonly held value – advancement of knowledge. Moreover, they perceived a system of double consent to be at work: the victim also had entered into the contract with the experimental authority and was not free to renounce his obligations unilaterally. Moreover, the argument goes, the victim had entered into the authority system of the experimenter without placing any prior conditions on how he was to be treated. He must, therefore, accept the consequences of his own freely made decision. However unpleasant the experience might be for him, contractual obligations must be honoured. Society is built on this presupposition.

This argument occurred with sufficient frequency to justify an empirical test. The idea was to alter the victim's mode of entry into the experiment, so that he did not, by implication or otherwise, consent to be shocked against his will.

Only a minor alteration in the procedure was required to achieve this. It is to be recalled that both putative subjects were informed of the nature of the learning experiment even before the learner was strapped into the electric chair and even before the first shock was administered. Following this, subjects signed a general release form, which stated: 'In participating in this experimental research of my own free will, I release Yale University and its employees from any legal claims arising from my participation'.

Typically, this release was handled as a matter of routine, but in the present experiment, after the drawing is held and the experiment is outlined, the learner demurs. Hovering over the release form, pen in hand, he states that because of his heart condition he can agree to be in the experiment only on the condition that the experiment be halted on his demand. 'I'll agree to be in it, but only on condition that you let me out when I say so; that's the only condition.' The experimenter, as well as the naïve subject, clearly hear this precondition, and the experimenter grunts in a mildly positive manner. The learner signs the release and is strapped into the electric chair. The learner has thus predefined the limits of his cooperation. The experiment proceeds.

When the learner protests at 150 volts, the experimenter disregards him and instructs the naïve subject to go on, as he had done in all previous conditions. An element of betrayal and patent injustice was thus introduced. The empirical question is whether it made a difference. Or is the 'contract' argument merely a philosophic issue remote from the real forces at work in the situation?

About a quarter of the defiant subjects specifically raised the point that the victim had attached conditions to his participation, and they used this point as an argument for disobedience:

> SUBJECT: He did say he wanted to be released if there was any trouble . . . I just can't listen to any more of that regardless of what you say about tissue damage.' [Disobedient at level 18]
>
> SUBJECT: We should respect his wishes; he wants to be let out, so we have to. You said he could get out when he wanted to. I know I'd want to be let out when I wanted to be.' [Disobedient at level 10]
>
> SUBJECT : I don't want to go on, I can't go on with this. It's against my grain to inflict pain on somebody. This man may be in mortal danger as far as I'm concerned. . . . I feel there is this, too, namely, the man agreed only if he would be permitted to leave and he signed with this understanding. I feel in all fairness to him we shouldn't continue, his having signed it that way. . . .' [Disobedient at level 12]

The majority of defiant subjects, however, did not make explicit reference to the contract, though there is evidence in their heightened concern with the 'legalities' of the experiment that they were aware of it. Consider the remarks of the following subject, a thirty-six-year-old salesman:

> SUBJECT [195 volts administered]: No, wait just a second. What is the liability involved here? Legal liability, I'm speaking of. I don't believe you do have the right to keep him in there if he doesn't want to continue.
>
> EXPERIMENTER: Although the shocks may be painful, there is no permanent tissue damage.
>
> SUBJECT: That isn't the answer. If the man doesn't want to go on, that's his business.
>
> EXPERIMENTER: The experiment requires that you continue.
>
> SUBJECT: The experiment from Yale's viewpoint, but not from a legal angle or his viewpoint. And in this case, I'm

just as legally obligated as you are if any damage comes to the person. . . .

SUBJECT [270 volts administered]: No, I don't want any more of this. . . . I understand what you're trying to do, but I also understand his rights.

[Subject breaks off.]

These comments should not obscure the over-all results of the experiment, which are shown in Table 3.

These findings show that the social contract doctrine is a feeble determinant of behaviour. Sixteen of the 40 subjects continued to obey the experimenter to the end of the board, disregarding the contractual limitation the victim had attached to his participation. This is to be compared with the 20 subjects who continued to obey in the relevant control, condition 6. There is some increment in disobedience, but it could easily represent a chance variation. Subjects were aware of the injustice being done to the victim, but they allowed the experimenter to handle the issue as he saw fit.

Experiment 10: Institutional Context

In psychophysics, animal learning, and other branches of psychology, the fact that measures are obtained at one institution rather than another is irrelevant to the interpretation of the findings, so long as the technical facilities for measurement are adequate and the operations are carried out with competence.

But it cannot be assumed that this holds true for the present study. The effectiveness of the experimenter's commands may depend on the institutional context in which they are issued. The experiments described thus far were conducted at Yale University, an organisation which most subjects regarded with respect and sometimes awe. In postexperimental interviews several participants remarked that the locale and sponsorship of the study gave them confidence in the integrity, competence, and benign purposes of the personnel; many indicated that they would not have shocked the learner if the experiments had

Site of Bridgeport experiments (building left of Austin's)

Fig. 10

Bridgeport site

been done elsewhere.

The issue of background authority had to be considered in interpreting the results that had been obtained thus far; moreover, it is highly relevant to any theory of human obedience. Consider how closely our compliance with the imperatives of others is tied to particular institutions and locales in our day-to-day activities. On request, we expose our throats to a man with a razor blade in the barbershop, but would not do so in a shoe store; in the latter setting we willingly follow the clerk's request to stand in our stockinged feet, but resist the command in a bank. In the laboratory of a great university, subjects may comply with a set of commands that would be resisted if given elsewhere. *One must always question the relationship of obedience to a person's sense of the context in which he is operating.*

To explore the problem we moved our apparatus to an office building in a nearby industrial city, Bridgeport, and replicated experimental conditions without any visible tie to the university.

Bridgeport subjects were invited to the experiment through a mail circular similar to the one used in the Yale study, with appropriate changes in letterhead, etc. As in the earlier study, subjects were paid $4.50 for coming to the laboratory. The same age and occupational distributions used at Yale and the identical personnel were employed.

The purpose in relocating in Bridgeport was to assure a complete dissociation from Yale, and in this regard we were fully successful. On the surface, the study appeared to be conducted by Research Associates of Bridgeport, an organisation of unknown character (the title had been concocted exclusively for use in this study).

The experiments were conducted in a three-room office suite in a somewhat rundown commercial building located in the downtown shopping area. The laboratory was sparsely furnished, though clean, and marginally respectable in appearance. When subjects inquired about professional affiliations, they were informed only that we were a private firm conducting research for industry.

Some subjects displayed scepticism concerning the motives of the Bridgeport experimenter. One man gave us a written account of the thoughts he experienced at the control board:

. . .Should I quit this damn test? Maybe he passed out? What dopes we were not to check up on this deal. How do we know that these guys are legit? No furniture, bare walls, no telephone. We could of called the Police up or the Better Business Bureau. I learned a lesson tonight. How do I know that Mr Williams [the experimenter] is telling the truth? . . . I wish I knew how many volts a person could take before lapsing into unconsciousness . . .

Another subject stated:

I questioned on my arrival my own judgment [about coming]. I had doubts as to the legitimacy of the operation and the consequences of participation. I felt it was a heartless way to conduct memory or learning processes on human beings and certainly dangerous without the presence of a medical doctor.

There was no noticeable reduction in tension for the Bridgeport subjects. And the subjects' estimation of the amount of pain felt by the victim was slightly, though not significantly, higher than in the Yale study.

A failure to obtain complete obedience in Bridgeport would indicate that the extreme compliance found in New Haven subjects was tied closely to the background authority of Yale University; if a large proportion of the subjects remained fully obedient, very different conclusions would be called for.

As it turned out, the level of obedience in Bridgeport, although somewhat reduced, was not significantly lower than that obtained at Yale. A large proportion of the Bridgeport subjects were fully obedient to the experimenter's commands (48 percent of the Bridgeport subjects delivered the maximum shock versus 65 percent in the corresponding condition at Yale), as Table 3 shows.

How are these findings to be interpreted? It is possible that if commands of a potentially harmful or destructive sort are to be perceived as legitimate they must occur within some sort of institutional structure. But it is clear from the study that it need not be a particularly reputable or distinguished institution. The Bridgeport experiments were conducted by an unimpressive firm lacking any credentials. The laboratory was set up in a respectable office building with its title listed in the building directory; otherwise there was no evidence of benevolence or competence. It is possible that the *category* of institution, judged according to its professed function, rather than its qualitative position within that category, wins our compliance. Persons deposit money in elegant, but also in seedy-looking banks, without giving much thought to the differences in security they offer. Similarly, our subjects may consider one laboratory to be as competent as another, so long as it is a scientific laboratory.

It would be valuable to pursue the investigation in contexts that go even further than the Bridgeport study in denying institutional support to the experimenter. It is possible that beyond a certain point obedience would disappear completely. But that point was not reached in the Bridgeport office: almost half the subjects obeyed the experimenter fully.

Experiment 11: Subject Free to Choose Shock Level

In the experiments described thus far the subject has acted in response to command, and we have assumed that the command is the effective cause of his action. But this conclusion is not warranted until we have performed a vital experimental control. For it is possible that the command is superfluous, that it simply corresponds to what the subject would do on his own.

Indeed, one theoretical interpretation of the behaviour holds that men harbour deeply aggressive instincts continually pressing for expression and that the experiment provides institutional justification for the release of these impulses. According to this view, if a person is placed in a situation where he has complete power over another individual, whom he may punish as much as he likes, all that is sadistic and bestial in man comes to the fore. The impulse to shock the victim is seen to flow from the potent aggressive tendencies, which are part of the motivational life of the individual, and the experiment, because it provides social legitimation, simply opens the door to their expression.

It becomes vital, therefore, to compare the subjects' performance when they are under orders and when they are allowed to choose the shock levels.

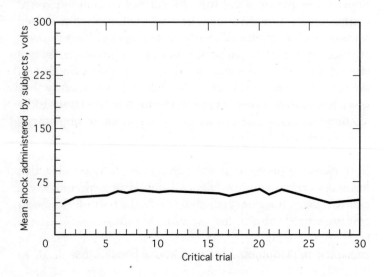

Fig. 11 Mean shock on each trial when subjects are free to choose levels. (A clinical trial refers to each occasion when the learner errs and incurrs a shock. There are thirty critical trials in the course of a laboratory hour.)

The procedure was identical to that used in Experiment 5 except that the teacher was told that he was free to select any shock level on any of the trials. (The experimenter took pains to point out that the teacher could use the highest levels on the generator, the lowest, any in between, or any combination of levels.) Each subject proceeded for thirty critical trials. The learner's protests were coordinated to standard shock levels, his first grunt coming at shock level 5, his first vehement protest at level 10. The results of the experiment are shown in Table 3.

The average (mean) shocks used across the thirty critical trials are shown in Figure 11, with an over-all average of 3.6. (It is to be recalled that the victim indicated no signs of discomfort at all until shock level 5.) We may also consider the maximum shock delivered by each subject (even if he used it only once and at any point in his performance). Three subjects limited their shocks to the very lowest on the board, 28 went no higher than the first indication of discomfort, and 38 did not go beyond the point where the learner vehemently protested (shock level 10). Two subjects provided the exception, administering the 25th and the 30th shock levels. But the over-all result was that the great majority of subjects delivered the very lowest shocks to the victim when the choice was left up to them.

We must always keep this result in mind in interpreting the meaning of these experiments. It is not enough to say that the situation provided a setting in which it was acceptable for the subject to hurt another person. This setting remained the same in the present experiment, and, by and large, subjects were not inclined to have the victim suffer. Insofar as the experiments tell us something about human nature, the revelation on how men act toward others when they are on their own is here. Whatever leads to shocking the victim at the highest level cannot be explained by autonomously generated aggression but needs to be explained by the transformation of behaviour that comes about through obedience to orders.

CHAPTER 7

INDIVIDUALS CONFRONT AUTHORITY II

Let us now consider the performance of several subjects who participated in the variations just described.

Fred Prozi, Unemployed (in Experiment 5)

The subject is about fifty years old, dressed in a jacket but no tie; he has a good-natured, if slightly dissolute, appearance. He employs working-class grammar and strikes one as a rather ordinary fellow.

He begins the experiment calmly but becomes increasingly tense as the experiment proceeds. After administering the 180-volt shock, he pivots around in his chair and, shaking his head, addresses the experimenter in agitated tones:

SUBJECT: I can't stand it. I'm not going to kill that man in there. You hear him hollering?

EXPERIMENTER: As I told you before, the shocks may be painful, but –

SUBJECT: But he's hollering. He can't stand it. What's going to happen to him?

EXPERIMENTER [his voice is patient, matter-of-fact]: The experiment requires that you continue, Teacher.

SUBJECT: Aaah, but, unh, I'm not going to get that man sick in there . . . know what I mean?

EXPERIMENTER: Whether the learner likes it or not, we must go on, through all the word pairs.

SUBJECT: I refuse to take the responsibility. He's in there hollering!

EXPERIMENTER: It's absolutely essential that you continue, Teacher.

SUBJECT [indicating the unused questions]: There's too many

left here; I mean, Geez, if he gets them wrong, there's too many of them left. I mean who's going to take the responsibility if anything happens to that gentleman?

EXPERIMENTER: I'm responsible for anything that happens to him. Continue, please.

SUBJECT: All right. [Consults list of words] The next one's 'Slow – walk, truck, dance, music'. Answer, please. [A buzzing sound indicates the learner has signalled his answer.] Wrong. A hundred and ninety-five volts. 'Dance'.

LEARNER [yelling]: Let me out of here. My heart's bothering me!

[Teacher looks at experimenter.]

EXPERIMENTER: Continue, please.

LEARNER [screaming]: Let me out of here, you have no right to keep me here. Let me out of here, let me out, my heart's bothering me, let me out! [Subject shakes head, pats the table nervously.]

SUBJECT: You see, he's hollering. Hear that? Gee, I don't know.

EXPERIMENTER: The experiment requires. . .

SUBJECT [interrupting]: I know it does, sir, but I mean – hunh! He don't know what he's getting in for. He's up to 195 volts!

[Experiment continues, through 210 volts, 225 volts, 240 volts, 255 volts, 270 volts, at which point the teacher, with evident relief, runs out of word-pair questions.]

EXPERIMENTER: You'll have to go back to the beginning of that page and go through them again until he's learned them all correctly.

SUBJECT: Aw, no. I'm not going to kill that man. You mean I've got to keep going up with the scale? No sir. He's hollering in there. I'm not going to give him 450 volts.

EXPERIMENTER: The experiment requires that you go on.

SUBJECT: I know it does, but that man is hollering in there, sir.

EXPERIMENTER [same matter-of-fact tone]: As I said before, although the shocks may be painful. . .

SUBJECT [interrupting]: Awwww. He – he – he's yelling in

there.

EXPERIMENTER: Start with 'Blue', please, at the top of the page. Continue, please, Teacher. Just go ahead.

SUBJECT [concentrating intently on the list of words in front of him, as if to shut everything else out]: 'Blue – boy, girl, grass, hat'. [Buzz indicates answer.] Correct. 'Night – day, sky, job, chair'. [Buzz] Wrong. The answer is 'day'. Two hundred and eighty-five volts.

LEARNER: Ohhuhhoohhh!

EXPERIMENTER: Continue, please.

SUBJECT: 'Fat – man, lady, tub, neck'. Answer, please. [Buzz] Wrong. The answer is 'neck'. Three hundred volts.

LEARNER: Ohhh. I absolutely refuse to answer any more. [Shouting urgently, now] Let me out of here. You can't hold me here. Get me out. Get – me – out – of – here.

EXPERIMENTER: Continue. The next word is 'Green', please.

SUBJECT: 'Green – grass, hat, ink, apple'. [Nothing happens. No answering buzz. Just gloomy silence.]

SUBJECT: I don't think he is going to answer.

EXPERIMENTER: If the learner doesn't answer in a reasonable time, about four or five seconds, consider the answer wrong. And follow the same procedures you have been doing for wrong answers. Say 'Wrong', tell him the number of volts, give him the punishment, read him the correct answer. Continue, please.

SUBJECT: 'Green – grass, hat, ink, apple'. Answer, please. [More silence. Subject just sits there.]

EXPERIMENTER: Go on with the procedure, please, Teacher.

SUBJECT: Three hundred and fifteen volts. The answer is 'ink'.

LEARNER: Ohh. Ooohh.

SUBJECT [relieved to hear response]: Next one.

LEARNER: I absolutely refuse to answer.

SUBJECT: You got to. You get a shock if you don't answer. [Experiment continues with learner refusing to answer, and, finally, failing even to grunt or groan. At 375 volts, the subject stands up.]

SUBJECT: I think something's happened to that fellow in there. I don't get no answer. He was hollering at less voltage. Can't you check in and see if he's all right, please?

EXPERIMENTER [with same detached calm]: Not once we've started. Please continue, Teacher.

SUBJECT [sits down, sighs deeply]: 'Cool – day, shade, water, paint'. Answer, please. Are you all right in there? Are you all right?

EXPERIMENTER: Please continue, Teacher. Continue, please. [Subject pushes lever.]

SUBJECT [swivelling around in his chair]: Something's happened to that man in there. [Swivelling back] Next one. 'Low – dollar, necklace, moon, paint'. [Turning around again] Something's happened to that man in there. You better check in on him, sir. He won't answer or nothing.

EXPERIMENTER: Continue. Go on, please.

SUBJECT: You accept all responsibility?

EXPERIMENTER: The responsibility is mine. Correct. Please go on.

[Subject returns to his list, starts running through words as rapidly as he can read them, works through to 450 volts.]

SUBJECT: That's that.

EXPERIMENTER: Continue using the 450-volt switch for each wrong answer. Continue, please.

SUBJECT: But I don't get no anything!

EXPERIMENTER: Please continue. The next word is 'white'.

SUBJECT: Don't you think you should look in on him, please?

EXPERIMENTER: Not once we've started the experiment.

SUBJECT: But what if something has happened to the man?

EXPERIMENTER: The experiment requires that you continue. Go on, please.

SUBJECT: Don't the man's health mean anything?

EXPERIMENTER: Whether the learner likes it or not...

SUBJECT: What if he's dead in there? [Gestures toward the room with the electric chair.] I mean, he told me he can't stand the shock, sir. I don't mean to be rude, but I think you should look in on him. All you have to do is look in on him. All you have to do is look in the door. I don't get no answer, no noise. Something might have happened to the gentleman in there, sir.

EXPERIMENTER: We must continue. Go on, please.

SUBJECT: You mean keep giving him what? Four-hundred fifty volts, what he's got now?

EXPERIMENTER: That's correct. Continue. The next word is 'white'.

SUBJECT [now at a furious pace]: 'White – cloud, horse, rock, house'. Answer, please. The answer is 'horse'. Four-hundred and fifty volts. [Administers shock.] Next word, 'Bag – paint, music, clown, girl'. The answer is 'paint'. Four-hundred and fifty volts. [Administers shock.] Next word is 'Short – sentence, movie'. . .

EXPERIMENTER: Excuse me, Teacher. We'll have to discontinue the experiment.

The subject's performance more or less speaks for itself, but we may note a few points. First, despite his numerous, agitated objections, his continuous and persistent dissent, he continues to administer the shocks as ordered by the experimenter. There is, thus, a dissociation between words and action. Second, by no stretch of the imagination can it be said that this man wanted to administer shocks to the learner. To the contrary, it was a painful act for him, one which came about because of his relationship to the experimenter. Third, we note that 'responsibility' is an issue important to the subject, and it is only when the experimenter explicitly accepts responsibility that, after several seconds of hesitation, the subject is able to continue. Finally, the language employed by the participant is revealing. Despite the considerable tension of the situation, a tone of courtesy and deference is meticulously maintained. The subject's objections strike us as inordinately weak and inappropriate in view of the events in which he is immersed. He thinks he is killing someone, yet he uses the language of the tea table.

Karen Dontz, Nurse (in Experiment 8)

Karen Dontz describes herself as a forty-year-old housewife who for the past six years has worked part time as a registered nurse. Her husband is a plumber. She is Catholic and her mother was born in Czechoslovakia. Mrs Dontz has an unusually casual, slow-paced way of speaking, and her tone expresses constant humility; it is as if every assertion carries the emotional message: 'I'm just a very ordinary person, don't expect a lot from me'. Physically, she resembles Shirley Booth in the film *Come Back, Little Sheba*.

Throughout the experiment she is nervous.

At 225 volts, she turns to the experimenter, stating in a highly tentative voice designed not to offend, 'I hesitate to press these.'

When he instructs her to follow the procedure, she does so without further comment. But before administering the 345-volt shock, she points to the label, DANGER on the shock generator.

The experimenter remarks that although the shocks are painful they cause no permanent tissue damage. She accepts the experimenter's comment saying, 'I'll continue, providing it's not dangerous.' She sits on the edge of her seat, but her voice remains casual when reading the word pairs. When no sound is heard from the learner, she queries, 'Do I go right to the end, sir? I hope there's nothing wrong with him there.'

She begins to mumble to herself inaudibly. When the experimenter instructs her to continue using the 450-volt switch, she says in tones that are both concerned but exceedingly humble, 'What if there's something wrong with the man, sir?'

But she proceeds.

In the interview she is very slow in her responses, and even after she is told that the learner received no shocks, she still considers the experiment to be one of the effect of punishment on learning. She emphasises that she did what the experimenter told her to do and seems satisfied with her own compliance. She states she was nervous because she knows that 210 volts (sic) is household current and 'most people can be electrocuted with that'. She emphasises she was more nervous here than in the hospital because 'in the hospital I know what rights I have; here, I didn't know'.

INTERVIEWER: Did you think of stopping at one time?

MRS DONTZ [in a lackadaisical tone]: He said, 'Go ahead.' I did. I said to him, 'I don't think I should go on any further.' He said, 'Go on with the experiment.'

INTERVIEWER: Is there anything Mr Wallace [the learner] could have said that would have caused you to stop the experiment?

MRS DONTZ: I don't think so.

Mrs Dontz points out that in a hospital nurses have a right to question a doctor's orders if they appear to be harmful to the patient.[7]

'If I question the dose of a drug, I can ask the doctor three times: "Is this the order you want? Is this the order you want?" And, if he keeps on saying "Go ahead," and I know this is above the average dose, I may call his attention to the fact that it's too much. It's not that you are better than he is, but you can say, "Did you want her to have so much, doctor," and then you repeat it. Then you still have the right to bring the question up to the supervisor.

In the experiment, she 'questioned' the voltage levels but was fully satisfied with the answers provided by the experimenter. Note that her most extreme response to the doctor's authority is to refer the issue to a supervisor. Moreover, it is clear that Mrs Dontz is routinely reviewing a hospital rulebook procedure, rather than describing her personal inclinations.

INTERVIEWER: Have you ever had occasion to do that in the hospital?

MRS DONTZ: Yes, I had.

INTERVIEWER: Often?

MRS DONTZ: No, very, very rarely. In fact, I've been working now the past six years. I think one time I just questioned the dosage.

INTERVIEWER: How did the screams sound to you? Did they sound real?

MRS DONTZ: Oh, yes! I was really concerned with the man in there. Worried he had a heart attack. He said he had a bad heart. Yes, I know that's a possibility.

Mrs Dontz is an unassuming person, of benign disposition, whose manner is that of a worn-out housewife. She does not argue. She carries out her hospital duties reliably and with a minimum of fuss. She possesses a soft manner from which her patients and the staff physicians benefit. Her relationship with authority is not problematical. For she has chosen to work in the nurturant environment of a hospital, in which there is congruence between her benign nature and the demands made on her by authority.

At the conclusion of the interview, Mrs Dontz perks up, and inquires, 'May I ask you, did any of the men go through and follow the 450 volts?'

The interviewer says he would be interested in her opinion on the matter. She replies, 'No, I don't think men would comply.'

Elinor Rosenblum, Housewife (in Experiment 8)

Mrs Rosenblum takes pleasure in describing her background: she graduated from the University of Wisconsin more than twenty years ago, and her husband, a film distributor, attended Dartmouth. She does volunteer work with juvenile delinquents once a week and has been active in the local Girl Scout organisation and the PTA. She is fluent and garrulous and projects herself strongly, with many references to her social achievements. She displays a pleasant though excessively talkative charm.

At the beginning of the experiment she claims to know nothing about electricity and is wary of the sample shock. In carrying out her task, she attempts to project an image of competence and social grace but is soon swept up in the experimental conflict. She maintains a pretentiously correct, almost authoritative tone in reading the word pairs to the learner, which contrast with the weak, girlish comments she directs to the experimenter. She expresses increasing concern as she moves up the voltage scale. At 270 volts she signals the correct answer to the learner by emphasising it vocally. While continuing to read the word pairs with a show of outward strength, she mutters in a tone of helplessness to the experimenter, 'Must I go on? Oh, I'm worried about him. Are we going all the way up there [pointing to the higher end of the generator]? Can't we stop? I'm shaking. I'm shaking. Do I have to go up there?'

She regains her composure temporarily but then cannot prevent periodic outbursts of distress. She mutters to herself, 'I'm shaking here,' yet her communication with the learner continues in the same officious tone. It is almost as if she were two women, one giving a competent public performance, and the other an inner, distressed woman unable to refrain from anxious utterances. She proceeds to the end of the board, administering the 450-volt shock three times. In the interview she says the shocks administered to the learner were extremely painful. When the experimenter asks her, 'What is the highest shock you would be willing to take as a sample?' she replies indignantly, 'Fifteen volts. I don't even think it's necessary. Fifteen, if I were to get any, and I wouldn't even want that. I don't think it's necessary.'

INTERVIEWER: Were you tense or nervous?

MRS ROSENBLUM: Extremely.

INTERVIEWER: Do you remember when you were most tense or nervous?

MRS ROSENBLUM: When he started screaming, 'Let me out of here.' How can I inflict punishment on a person like that? I was shaking. I didn't even know what I was reading. I'm still shaking. I'm nervous because I was hurting him.

She was nervous not because the man was being hurt but because *she* was performing the action. Similarly, while administering shock, she asserts her own distress to be the main reason for terminating the experiment. A self-centred quality permeates her remarks.

She spontaneously offers the following account of her volunteer work, recounted with enormous zest:

MRS ROSENBLUM: I work at Farrel High School, with dropouts. They are all more or less leather-jacket guys. They're my boys. I'm trying to teach them to stay in school, and further their study . . . but I don't do it with punishment, I do it with attention and with *love*. As a matter of fact, they regard it as a privilege at this point to go with me. Whereas at the beginning they just did it to get away from school and to have a cigarette. But they don't do it any more. I've gotten everything from them through love and kindness. But *never* through punishment.

INTERVIEWER: What do you teach them?

MRS ROSENBLUM: Well, first of all, I teach them manners. That's the first thing I had to do; teach them respect for people, respect for older people, respect for girls their age, respect for society. This is the first thing I had to do before I could teach them anything else. Then I could teach them to make something of themselves, and go after so-called luxuries.

The importance she attaches to respect for society is not unrelated to her own submissive manner of relating to the experimenter. And a conventional outlook permeates her thinking.

Her dialogue is filled with feminine references:

MRS ROSENBLUM: I have gotten so much through love, and I have a wonderful daughter. She's fifteen, and she's National Honour Society: a *bright* girl. And a *wonderful* child. But all through *love*, not through punishment. Oh God, no!

The worst thing you can do is . . . with punishment. The only time punishment is good is with an infant.

INTERVIEWER: What did you think of the experiment?

MRS ROSENBLUM [She does not allow the question to change her former train of thought]: I don't believe you'll get anything from punishment; only with an infant where they have no mind. When my daughter was little I punished her for three things. As a matter of fact, I let her punish herself. I let her touch a hot stove. She burned herself and she never touched it again.

INTERVIEWER: Let me tell you a little about the experiment. First, Mr Wallace did not receive any shocks.

MRS ROSENBLUM : You're kidding! He didn't get what I got. [She squeals] I can't *believe* this. You mean to say this was all in his *mind*!

EXPERIMENTER: Oh no, he is an employee of Yale, an actor.

MRS ROSENBLUM : Every time I pressed the button, I died. Did you see me shaking. I was just dying here to think that I was administering shocks to this poor man.

[The learner is brought in. She turns to him.]

MRS ROSENBLUM : You're an actor, boy. You're marvellous! Oh, my God, what he [the experimenter] did to me. I'm exhausted. I didn't want to go on with it. You don't know what I went through here. A person like me hurting you, my God. I didn't want to do it to you. Forgive me, please. I can't get over this. My face is beet red. I wouldn't hurt a fly. I'm working with boys, trying to teach them, and I'm getting such marvellous results, *without* punishment. I said to myself at the beginning, I don't feel you'll get anything by inflicting punishment.

We note, however, recalling how she allowed her daughter to touch the hot stove, that she is not against punishment per se but only against her active infliction of it. If it just 'happens', it is acceptable.

She confides to the learner, 'As a matter of fact I tried to push the switch down very lightly. Did you hear me *stressing* the word. I was hoping that you would hear me.'

INTERVIEWER: Isn't this similar to what a nurse has to do, if a doctor instructs her to administer a needle?

MRS ROSENBLUM: I'm the most *marvellous* person in an emergency. I will do whatever has to be done regardless of who I hurt. And I don't shake. But I will do it without thinking. I won't even hesitate.

This more or less parallels her behaviour in the laboratory.

MRS ROSENBLUM: I kept saying, 'For what reason am I hurting this poor man?'

INTERVIEWER: *Why* did you go on?

MRS ROSENBLUM: It is an experiment. I'm here for a reason. So I had to do it. You said so. I didn't want to. I'm very interested in this . . . this whole project. May I ask you something? Do you have a moment? How do other people react?

EXPERIMENTER: How do you think?

MRS ROSENBLUM: Well, I tell you. The choice of me as a woman doing this . . . you certainly picked a pip. In my volunteer work, there aren't many women who will do what I do. . . . I'm unusual; I'm softhearted, I'm a softy. I don't know how I as a woman stand in relation to the other women; they're a little harder than I am. I don't think they care too much.

I was tempted so much to stop and to say: 'Look I'm not going to do it anymore. Sorry. I'm not going to do it'. I kept saying that to myself, 'Sorry, I'm just not going to do it.' Then he kept quiet. And I thought maybe he's in shock, because he said he had a heart condition. But I knew you wouldn't let anything happen to him. So I went on with it, *much* against my will. I was going through hell. . . . I don't think others would be as nervous as I. . . . I don't think they would care too much. With the way they are with their children I don't think they really care too much about other people.

She construes her expressions of tension purely as a sign of virtue: she was nervous because she cared about the victim. She insists on talking about herself. The experimenter listens patiently.

MRS ROSENBLUM: I sometimes say to myself, 'Why don't you take a job as president of Woman's Assembly, and get acclaim, honour, newspapers, prestige enough to burn, instead of working with my leather-jacketed guys with absolutely no publicity?' Doing it once a week. This is the story of my life; I was a scout mother for five years. It ended with thirty girls in my troop and everyone begging to get into it. But I couldn't because there's a limit. I'm much relieved now. I'm one for science; this is what I wanted to study, anyway. I'm trying to get my daughter to go into it. I'm very glad I did this; see how relaxed I am now?

The interview was continued until Mrs Rosenblum seemed sufficiently calm to be discharged from the laboratory.

Mrs Rosenblum is a person whose psychic life lacks integration. She has not been able to find life purposes consistent with her needs for esteem and success. Her goals, thinking, and emotions are fragmented. She carried out her experimental role as teacher showing great outward conviction, while at the same time she displayed another side of herself to the experimenter, behaving meekly and submissively.

It is not surprising that she failed to mobilise the psychic resources needed to translate her compassion for the learner into the disobedient act. Her feelings, goals, and thoughts were too diverse and unintegrated.

All evidence indicates that at the time of her performance she believed the learner was being shocked. But it is not difficult for a woman of hysterical tendencies to adjust her thinking in a manner consistent with a positive self-image. In a questionnaire returned to us a few months later, she states that during the experiment her 'mature and well-educated brain' had not believed the learner was getting shocks. Through a post-facto adjustment of thought, she protects her cherished – if unrealistic – picture of her own nature.

Gretchen Brandt, Medical Technician (in Experiment 8)

The subject is an attractive thirty-one-year-old medical technician who works at the University Medical School. She had emigrated from Germany five years before and speaks with a thick German accent.

On several occasions, when the learner complains, she turns to the experimenter coolly and inquires, 'Shall I continue?' She promptly returns to her task when the experimenter asks her to do so. At the administration of 210 volts, she turns to the experimenter, remarking firmly, 'Well, I'm sorry, I don't think we should continue.'

EXPERIMENTER: The experiment requires that you go on until he has learned all the word pairs correctly.

GRETCHEN: He has a heart condition, I'm sorry. He told you that before.

EXPERIMENTER: The shocks may be painful but they are not dangerous.

GRETCHEN: Well, I'm sorry, I think when shocks continue like this, they *are* dangerous. You ask him if he wants to get out. It's his free will.

EXPERIMENTER: It is absolutely essential that we continue...

GRETCHEN: I like you to ask him. We came here of our free will. If he wants to continue I'll go ahead. He told you he had a heart condition. I'm sorry. I don't want to be responsible for anything happening to him. I wouldn't like it for me either.

EXPERIMENTER: You have no other choice.

GRETCHEN: I think we here are on our own free will. I don't want to be responsible if he has a heart condition if anything happens to him. Please understand that.

She refuses to go further and the experiment is terminated.

The woman is firm and resolute throughout. She indicates in the interview that she was in no way tense or nervous, and this corresponds to her controlled appearance throughout. She feels that the last shock she administered to the learner was extremely painful and reiterates that she 'did not want to be responsible for any harm to him'. She listens to the experimenter's explanation in an interested fashion, expresses surprise that the learner was not being shocked, and indicates she will accept only 45 volts as a maximum sample shock.

The woman's straightforward, courteous behaviour in the experiment, lack of tension, and total control of her own action seems to make disobedience a simple and rational deed. Her behaviour is the very embodiment of what I had initially envisioned would be true for almost all subjects.

Ironically, Gretchen Brandt grew to adolescence in Hitler's Germany and was for the great part of her youth exposed to Nazi propaganda. When asked about the possible influence of her background, she remarks slowly, 'Perhaps we have seen too much pain.'

Pasqual Gino, Water Inspector (in Experiment 7)

Pasqual Gino is a forty-three-year-old water inspector who was born in the United States of Italian parents. He took part in the variation in which the experimenter, having given the subject and victim instructions, departs from the laboratory and leaves his telephone number. Thus, the subject is left alone with the victim in the laboratory, but is free to call the experimenter if problems arise. Mr Gino telephones the experimenter on several occasions. After administering 150 volts' shock, he calls to say 'Professor, this gentleman is complaining. He wants to get out. He does not want to take it no more . . . I just gave him 150 volts and he said, "That's it!"'

The experimenter instructs the subject by telephone to continue, and Mr Gino does so.

He remains alone in the experimental room, dutifully carrying out the instructions; meanwhile the victim protests strenuously. At the 300-volt level, when the victim refuses to provide answers, Mr Gino telephones the experimenter again and once more the experimenter tells him to go on, saying that the absence of an answer is to be treated as a wrong answer.

'You want me to go right to the end of the board on the voltage? Uh huh, and when I get to the end, what do I do?'

After 330 volts, no further utterance is heard from the victim either in protest or pain. Concerned, Mr Gino again telephones:

'Professor, I don't hear any noise in there now at all. I'm up to 330 volts. I don't hear any whimper or anything and I'm kind of leery about this thing. Do you think something happened to the gentleman?'

The experimenter asserts that though the shocks may be painful, there is no permanent tissue damage. The subject again returns to his task, alone in the laboratory room. After he administers the 450-volt level, he calls the experimenter, again reminding him that no sound is emanating from the learner.

In time, the experimenter returns to the laboratory and informs Mr Gino that the learner is unharmed. In the interview, when asked about the degree of tension he felt, he answered: 'I was more nervous for the other gentleman than I was for myself. ... I was more nervous for him. I was nervous because you were not here. If you were here I wouldn't have been nervous at all. I mean, if that man should have passed out with me giving him these things, these shocks – well, I'd feel that I'm responsible on account of me – giving these shocks.'

The subject accepts responsibility not in a general philosophic way but only feels that the situation seemed to focus responsibility on him because he was alone with the learner. He goes on: '[If you had been here] you'd say, "Let's stop it" or "Let's continue" or something. You know better than I. You're the professor. I'm not. . . . But, on the other hand, I got to say that the last I know of him was around 255 volts and that was the last he complained.' [The subject then mimics the complaints of the learner.]

Several months after his performance in the experiment, Mr Gino took part in a group discussion of his experience. In retrospect, he considered the experiment 'terrific'. 'I was fascinated with it [and] . . . that night I went to a party; I have a couple of sisters-in-law that are nurses, you know, and they were fascinated with it, too. . . . I'm telling you it's something I'll never forget as long as I live.'

The experiment, even months after, seemed never to have raised in him the question of whether or not he should have considered disobeying the instructions to continue giving shocks.

'. . . I had about eight more levels to pull and he [the learner] was really hysterical in there and he was going to get the police, and what not. So I called the professor three times. And the third time he said, "Just continue," so I give him the next jolt. And then I don't hear no more answer from him, not a whimper or anything. I said, "Good God, he's dead; well, here we go, we'll finish him." And I just continued all the way through to 450 volts.'

Mr Gino does not object to taking the orders, although he suggests he would have been more comfortable if the instructor had been present in the laboratory with him. When asked if he had been bothered or disturbed because of giving the shocks, he said, 'No . . . I figured: well, this is an experiment, and Yale knows what's going on, and if they think it's all right, well, it's all right with me. They know more than I do. . . . I'll go through with anything they tell me to do.' He then explains:

'This is all based on a man's principle in life, and how he was brought up and what goals he sets in life. How he wants to carry on things. I know that when I was in the service, [If I was told] "You go over the hill, and we're going to attack," we attack. If the lieutenant says, "We're going to go on the firing range, you're going to crawl on your gut," you're going to crawl on your gut. And if you come across a snake, which I've seen a lot of fellows come across, copperheads, and guys were told not to get up, and they got up. And they got killed. So I think it's all based on the way a man was brought up in his background.'

In his story, although the copperheads were a real danger, and caused an instinctive reaction to stand, to do this violated the lieutenant's order to hug the ground. And in the end those who disobeyed were destroyed. Obedience, even in the face of trying circumstances, is the most reliable assurance of survival. At the close of the discussion, Mr Gino summarises his reaction to his own performance.

'Well, I faithfully believed the man was dead until we opened the door. When I saw him, I said, "Great, this is great." But it didn't bother me even to find that he was dead. I did a job.'

He reports that he was not disturbed by the experiment in the months just after it but was curious about it. When he received the final report, he relates telling his wife, 'I believe I conducted myself behaving and obediently, and carried on instructions as I always do. So I said to my wife, "Well here we are. And I think I did a good job." She said, "Suppose the man was dead?" '

Mr Gino replied, 'So he's dead. I did my job!'

CHAPTER 8

ROLE PERMUTATIONS

Thus far we have observed the subject's response to a situation which has been altered in roughly mechanical ways but whose basic structure has been retained intact. To be sure, varying the distance between subject and victim has important psychological effects, but a more far-reaching decomposition of the situation is necessary if the roots of this social behaviour are to be examined. Such a treatment will require not only movement of the victim from this side of the laboratory floor to that but also must proceed from an analysis of essential components, then seek their recombination in an altered situational chemistry.

Within the experimental setting, we find the three elements: *position, status*, and *action. Position* indicates whether the person prescribes, administers, or receives the shock. This is conceptually separable from the role of experimenter or subject, as we shall see. *Status* – treated as a two-valued attribute in this study – refers to whether the person is presented as an authority or an ordinary man. *Action* refers to the conduct of the person in each of the three positions, and more specifically to whether he advocates or opposes shocking the victim.

In the experiments reported thus far, all relations among these elements have remained invariant. *Action*, for example, has always been linked to a particular status. Thus, the person who received the shock has always been an ordinary man (as opposed to an authority), and his action has invariably been to protest the shock.

As long as the invariant relations among *position, action*, and *status* are retained, we cannot answer certain fundamental questions. For example, is the subject responding principally to the content of the command to shock or to the *status* of the

	Person I	Person II	Person III
Position:	Person who orders the shock	Person at the control board	Person who receives the shock
Status:	Authority	Ordinary man	Ordinary man
Action:	Advocates administration of shock	Indeterminate	Opposes shock
Specific name	"Experimenter"	Teacher	Learner
Conceptual referent	Authority	Subject	Victim

Fig. 12 Role permutations

person who issues it? Is it what is said or who says it that largely determines his actions?

Experiment 12: Learner Demands to Be Shocked

Let us begin with a reversal of imperatives between experimenter and victim:

Until now, the experimenter has always told the subject to go on with the shocks and the learner has always protested. In the first role permutation this will be reversed. It is the learner who will demand to be shocked, and the experimenter who will forbid shocking him.

This variation was performed as follows: The learner emitted cries of pain as he was shocked; yet, despite his discomfort, he appeared willing to go on. After the 150-volt shock was delivered, the experimenter called a halt to the study, stating that the learner's reactions were unusually severe and that, in view of his heart condition, no further shocks should be administered. The learner then cried out that he *wanted* to go on with the experiment, that a friend of his had recently been in the study and had gone to the end and that it would be an affront to his manliness to be discharged from the experiment. The experimenter replied that although it would be valuable for the study to continue, in view of the learner's reaction of pain, no further shocks were to be given. The learner persisted in demanding that the experiment continue, asserting that he had come to the laboratory 'to do a job' and that he intended to do it. He insisted that the teacher continue with the procedure. The subject thus faced a learner who demanded to be shocked and the experimenter who forbade it.

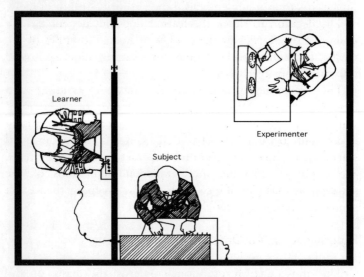

Fig. 13 Learner demands to be shocked

The results of the experiment are shown in Table 4. Not a single subject complied with the learner's demands; every subject stopped administering shocks upon the experimenter's order.

Subjects are willing to shock the learner on the authority's demand but not on the learner's demand. In this sense, they regard the learner as having less right over himself than the authority has over him. The learner has come to be merely part of a total system, which is controlled by the authority. It is not the substance of the command but its source in authority that is of decisive importance. In the basic experiment, when the experimenter says, 'Administer 165 volts,' most subjects do so despite the learner's protest. But when the learner himself says, 'Administer 165 volts,' not a single subject is willing to do so. And, of course, within the purposes defined by authority, it is not meaningful to do so, which merely demonstrates how thoroughly dominated by authority's purposes is the entire situation. The learner wants to go through the shock series to get to the personal satisfaction of displaying his manliness, but this personal wish is totally irrelevant in a situation in which the subject has thoroughly embraced the authority's point of view.

The decision to shock the learner does not depend on the wishes of the learner or the benign or hostile impulses of the subject, but rather on the degree to which the subject is bound into the authority system.

The reversal of imperatives between victim and experimenter constitutes an extreme alteration of the standard situation. It produces clearcut, if not altogether surprising effects; but too much has been changed relative to the usual situation to enable us to pinpoint the exact causes of the effects. We ought to examine more moderate alterations of the situation, so that even if the effects are less sweeping, their exact source can be more precisely specified.

Experiment 13: An Ordinary Man Gives Orders

The most critical question concerns the basis of the experimenter's power to induce the subject to shock the victim. Is it due to the content of the command per se, or does the potency of the command stem from the authoritative source from which it is issued? As pointed out, the experimenter's role possesses both a status component and a particular imperative to shock the victim. We may now eliminate the status component while retaining the imperative. The simplest way to do this is to remove the command from the experimenter and assign it to an ordinary person.[8]

The procedure in this variation allowed an ordinary man, who appears to be a subject, to order specific shock levels. Three

Table 4. Maximum Shocks Administered in Role-Permutation Experiments.

Shock level	Verbal designation and voltage level	Experiment 12: Learner Demands to Be Shocked (n = 20)	Experiment 13: Ordinary Man Gives Orders (n = 20)	Experiment 13a: Subject as Bystander (n = 16)
	Slight shock			
1	15			
2	30			
3	45			
4	60			
	Moderate Shock			
5	75			
6	90			
7	105		1	
8	120			
	Strong Shock			
9	135			
10	150	20	7	3
11	165		1	1
12	180			
	Very Strong Shock			
13	195		3	
14	210			
15	225			
16	240			
	Intense Shock			
17	255		1	
18	270		1	
19	285			
20	300		1	
	Extreme Intensity Shock			
21	315			
22	330			
23	345		1	
24	360			
	Danger : Severe Shock			
25	375			
26	390			
27	405			
28	420			1
	XXX			
29	435			
30	450		4	11
	Mean maximum shock level	10.0	16.25	24.9
	Percentage administering maximum shock	0.0%	20.0%	68.75%°

° Refers to the percentage of subjects, of the 16 who had defied the common man, who did not interfere with the common man's administration of the maximum shock.
See text.

Table 4. Maximum Shocks Administered in Role-Permutation Experiments.

Shock level	Verbal designation and voltage level	Experiment 14: Authority as Victim (n = 20)	Experiment 15: Two Authorities: Contradictory Commands (n = 20)	Experiment 16: Two Authorities One as Victim (n = 20)
	Slight shock			
1	15			
2	30			
3	45			
4	60			
	Moderate Shock			
5	75			
6	90			
7	105			
8	120			
	Strong Shock			
9	135		1	
10	150	20	18	6
11	165		1	
12	180			
	Very Strong Shock			
13	195			
14	210			
15	225			
16	240			
	Intense Shock			
17	255			
18	270			
19	285			
20	300			1
	Extreme Intensity Shock			
21	315			
22	330			
23	345			
24	360			
	Danger : Severe Shock			
25	375			
26	390			
27	405			
28	420			
	XXX			
29	435			
30	450			13
	Mean maximum shock level	10.0	10.0	23.5
	Percentage administering maximum shocks	0.0%†	0.0%	65.0%

† See text, p 101 for a meaning of this figure.

subjects (two of them accomplices of the experimenter) arrive at the laboratory, and through a rigged drawing the usual confederate is assigned the victim's role. The second confederate is assigned the task of recording times from a clock at the experimenters desk. The naïve subject, through the drawing, is assigned the job of reading the word pairs and administering shocks to the learner. The experimenter goes through the usual instructions, straps the victim into the electric chair, and administers sample shocks. However, at no point does the experimenter indicate which shock levels are to be

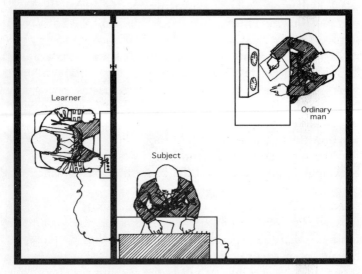

Fig. 14 An ordinary man gives orders

administered. A rigged telephone call takes the experimenter away from the laboratory. Somewhat flustered, but eager to have his experiment completed, the experimenter indicates before departing that the learning information will be recorded automatically and that the subjects should go on with the experiment until all the word pairs are learned perfectly (again, not mentioning which shock levels are to be used).

After the experimenter departs, the accomplice, with some enthusiasm, announces that he has just thought of a good system to use in administering the shocks, specifically, to increase the shock level one step each time the learner makes a mistake; throughout the experiment he insists that this procedure be followed.

Thus the subject is confronted with a general situation that has been defined by an experimental authority, but with orders on specific levels issued by an insistent, ordinary man who lacks any status as an authority.

Before proceeding with a discussion of the results, a few observations are needed on the over-all situation. First, the staging of this experiment was, of necessity, more strained than usual. The withdrawal of the experimenter from the laboratory was awkward and undermined the credibility of the situation in some degree. Second, although the aim of the experiment was to strip the commands of any authoritative source, it was almost impossible to do this in a completely effective manner. There were many traces of derived authority even when the experimenter was absent. The overall situation had been defined by the authority, as well as the idea of administering shocks. It was only the specification of exact shock levels that was reserved for the common man. Authority was hovering in the background and had created the basic situation in which the participants found themselves.

Nevertheless, there was a sharp drop in compliance: sixteen of the twenty subjects broke with the common man, despite his insistence that the experiment be continued and a continuous barrage of persuasive argument on his part. The scores are shown in Table 4. Only a third as many subjects followed the common man as follow the experimenter.

Before discussing the import of these results, let us move on to an extension of the experiment.

Experiment 13a: The Subject as Bystander

When the subject refused to go along with the common man's instructions, a new situation was introduced. The confederate, apparently disgusted by the refusal, would assert that if the other man was unwilling to do it, he personally would take over the administration of shocks. He then asked the subject to record the shock durations and he moved to a position in front of the shock generator. Thus the subject was relieved of personally administering shocks to the learner but witnessed a harrowing scene in which the aggressive co-participant single-mindedly pursued his plan of increasing the shock step by step. Of the sixteen subjects exposed to this situation, virtually all protested the actions of the co-participant; five took physical action against him, or the shock generator, to terminate the administration of shocks. (Several attempted to disconnect the generator from its electrical source; four physically restrained the co-participant.) One, a large man, lifted the zealous shocker from his chair, threw him to a corner of the laboratory, and did not allow him to move until he had promised not to administer further shocks. However passive subjects may have seemed when facing authority, in the present situation five of them rose heroically to the protection of the victim. They felt free to threaten the common man and were not reluctant to criticise his judgment or personally chastise him; their attitude contrasts sharply with the deferential politeness subjects invariably displayed in other experiments, when an authority was at the helm. There, even when subjects disobeyed, they maintained a courteous, even a deferential relationship to the authority. The breakoff points are shown in Table 4.

Here are the remarks of a subject at the point when the coparticipant suggests that he personally take over administration of shocks:

COMMON MAN: Want me to take over?

SUBJECT: You sit still! You don't take over anything I do.
[The subject tries to let the victim out of his room, but cannot because the door is locked. He indicates that he will look for the experimenter. The common man again suggests that more shocks be administered.]

SUBJECT : No – no more. [Shouts at the common man] I said NO! That means 'no!' You hurt him and . . . he wants out. I'm going to get the experimenter. You hurt him once more you'd better put your glasses down.

In refusing to go along with the common man, most subjects assume that they are doing what the experimenter would have wanted them to do. And when asked to give their impression of the common man, they remarked:

> 'He is the kind of fella that can pull switches all day long – as long as he's not on the other end. If he was alive in medieval days, he could probably be the guy who ran the wrack.'

> 'Too persistent. I wouldn't want to be his child. He kept insisting, "Let's go on and let's go on." . . . He just went down the line and said "I have a system." I thought it too tough.'

> 'I thought he was a little too cruel. He was shocking him even though he wasn't answering any more.'

But one of the four who had gone all the way under the common man's prodding said this of him:

> 'I thought he was a strong teacher. A capable teacher. By strong – he wouldn't take any fooling around. He had in mind a project, and it had to be done correctly, and this is the attitude that he took. I thought it was commendable for him to take this kind of attitude. As far as his capabilities – there was no question as to how we should run it. He seemed to work it all very well.'

Experiment 14:
Authority as Victim: An Ordinary Man Commanding

So far we have looked at the status of the person who orders shocks. Now let us consider the status of the person who receives the shocks.

This alteration follows logically if we are to exhaust the more important permutations of position and status. We need to note the effect of treating an authority as victim – that is, to insert the experimenter's status into the victim's position. But who then shall order the shocks, an authority or a common man? We shall describe both situations, but let us begin with the ordinary man commanding shocks against the authority.

In order to create a situation in which the authority could plausibly come to receive shocks on the instruction of an ordinary person, the following procedure was used. Two persons arrive at the laboratory and draw for the roles of teacher and learner. The experiment is conducted as usual up to the point where the experimenter begins to describe the punishment the learner may receive. At this point the learner expresses reluctance to go on, asserting he is afraid of shocks. He says,

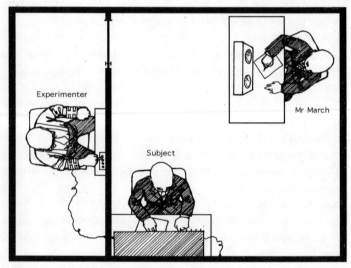

Fig. 15 Authority as victim: an ordinary man commanding

however, that if he could see someone else – the experimenter, for instance – go through the experiment just as he would have to, then he would be willing to continue. The experimenter, who has already indicated his extreme need for subjects and the difficulty of obtaining volunteers to be shocked, agrees to serve as the learner. He stipulates, though, that he is doing it on condition that the other will serve as learner immediately afterward. The experimenter is then strapped into the chair, the electrode paste applied, etc. The experiment proceeds with the subject administering shocks to the experimenter and the confederate seated at the experimenter's desk.

At 150 volts the experimenter demands to be let out, but the confederate insists forcefully that he go on according to the agreement. Thus the subject finds himself shocking an experimenter, who demands to be let out, while a common man insists that the shocks be continued, just as they would be in his case.

Considering the somewhat unusual nature of this experiment, it must be said that the procedure worked well, and was surprisingly plausible, in no small measure because of the excellent acting skills of the confederates.

Here is a transcript of one of the performances:

[They have just drawn lots. The naïve subject is the teacher. The confederate, Mr March, is to be the learner.]

EXPERIMENTER: The first thing we have to do is set the learner up so he can receive some kind of punishment. Please come with me into this next room.

MR MARCH: What do you mean by punishment?

EXPERIMENTER: Well, we have this machine, which is a shock generator. And the punishment we use is an electric shock.

MR MARCH: I would get the electric shock?

EXPERIMENTER: If you make mistakes in the lesson the teacher will be giving you.

MR MARCH: You mean like 15 volts, 30 volts?

EXPERIMENTER: Yes.

MR MARCH: He'll stay down here, I hope [pointing to lower level shocks].

EXPERIMENTER: Well, that depends on you, Mr March. It depends on the progress you make in the lesson.

MR MARCH: Well, would you go as high as 75 volts?

EXPERIMENTER: Possibly, yes. It depends on the number of mistakes. . . .

MR MARCH: Would you go as high as 120?

EXPERIMENTER: Yes, it's possible. . . .

MR MARCH: What's the most shock I might receive?

EXPERIMENTER: Well, this depends again on the progress

you make in the lesson.

MR MARCH: Just saying that I don't do too well, how much could I receive?

EXPERIMENTER: Well, it's conceivable that the teacher would have to go to the end of the board, if the experiment calls for this. But . . . this depends completely on the progress you . . . make in the lesson.

MR MARCH: I'm a little reluctant to take shocks that strong. I'm willing to do it down here [pointing to lower shocks]. You know, 15 volts.

EXPERIMENTER: To be frank, we've had some difficulty arranging enough people to volunteer for this particular experiment because of the shock.

MR MARCH: I can see why.

EXPERIMENTER: So much difficulty that I've been tempted to become a learner myself in one of these things. To be frank, we have to complete this condition by this evening. And we are short. If we don't have everyone cooperating with us and go through the experiment, we are not going to finish off the condition this evening. So, therefore, I would really appreciate your cooperation.

MR MARCH: If I could get some assurance. If you'd go through it first, for example, and you showed me that you could take the shocks, then I would definitely do it. If someone would show that he could take these shocks.

EXPERIMENTER: How about this, Mr March? If we run one experiment with me as the learner, would you then be willing to go through the experiment as the learner?

MR MARCH: If you went through it just the way I would have to go through it? Getting the shocks and all?

EXPERIMENTER: The whole business.

MR MARCH: If I saw you do it, and I saw you come out on your own two feet, I would do it.

EXPERIMENTER: All right, why don't we do that? Actually, this will help us out. It will be two experiments rather than one, and it will help us meet the quota by tonight. Why don't we do it that way, then? I will go through the experiment first. And as soon as I complete the

experiment, then you will be the learner. O.K.?

MR MARCH: Yeah.

EXPERIMENTER: OK, fine.

MR MARCH: If you go through it and you can take it, I can take it.

The experimenter gives additional instructions to the naïve subject seated at the shock generator; then he assists the experimenter by strapping him into the electric-chair apparatus, applying the electrode paste, etc. Here is the transcript beginning at the point when the experimenter demands to be let out:

[150 Volts administered]

EXPERIMENTER [shouts]: That's enough, gentlemen.

SUBJECT: I don't blame you.

MR MARCH: Oh, no, let's go on. Oh, no, come on, I'm going to have to go through the whole thing. Let's go. Come on, let's keep going.

SUBJECT [to the experimenter]: What do you say?

MR MARCH [interrupting]: He said I might have to take it to 450. I want to see if he can do it.

SUBJECT: The man can't take it, though. There's no sense in doing it, you know what I mean.

MR MARCH: Oh, no.

SUBJECT [to Mr March]: I'll let you call it quits anytime you want to. Right? How's that?

MR MARCH: He said we have to learn it perfectly.

SUBJECT: Now, I don't want to make the man suffer, now. Look, we're going up pretty high. You're going up to 165.

MR MARCH: He said you have to learn it perfectly. He said you could go up all the way.

SUBJECT: Well, I'll leave it up to him. If he don't want to, then we'll stop.

EXPERIMENTER: Please, let's call it off.

SUBJECT: All right.

[Subject immediately goes into cubicle where experimenter is strapped into chair and releases him. Mr

March continues insisting that the experiment go on.]

MR MARCH: Didn't you say to me that. . .

EXPERIMENTER: Regardless of what I said, I'm calling it off.

SUBJECT [warmly, as the experimenter is being released]: That's really something. I could feel those shocks myself. Every time I pushed that button. You were going up pretty high. You know the sample you gave me was pretty bad and that was, what? Seventy-five? And he went all the way up to 160.

Mr March's instructions to shock the experimenter were totally disregarded, as Table 4 shows. At the first protest of the shocked experimenter, every subject broke off, refusing to administer even a single shock beyond this point. There is no variation whatsoever in response. Further, many subjects literally leapt to the aid of the experimenter, running into the other room to unstrap him. Subjects often expressed sympathy for the experimenter, but appeared alienated from the common man, as if he were a madman.

Many subjects explained their prompt response on humane grounds, not recognising the authority aspect of the situation. Apparently, it is more gratifying for the subjects to see their action as stemming from personal kindness than to acknowledge that they were simply following the boss's orders. When asked what they would do if a common man were being shocked, these subjects vehemently denied that they would continue beyond the point where the victim protests; they do not correctly assess the weight of authority in their decision. Many of the actions that individuals take in daily life, which appear to them to flow from inner moral qualities, are no doubt similarly prompted by authority.

We have examined three experiments in which a common man, rather than an authority, instructs another individual to administer shocks. In the first experiment, the learner himself, to prove his manliness, demanded that the experiment be continued, while the experimenter called it to a halt. Not a single subject went along with the learner's demand to be shocked further. In the second experiment, in the absence of

the experimenter, but with his general blessings, a common man attempted to prescribe increasing shock levels for another participant, despite the victim's protests. Sixteen of the twenty subjects refused to follow him. In the third experiment, a common man ordered shocks against the authority. The moment the authority called a halt to the procedure, all subjects stopped immediately, totally disregarding the common man's callous orders.

These studies confirm an essential fact: the decisive factor is the response to authority, rather than the response to the particular order to administer shocks. Orders originating outside of authority lose all force. Those who argue that aggressive motives or sadistic instincts are unleashed when the command to hurt another person is given must take account of the subjects' adamant refusal to go on in these experiments. It is not what subjects do but for whom they are doing it that counts.

Double Authority

The focus of conflict thus far has been between an ordinary person and an authority. Let us now see what happens when authority itself is in conflict. In real life, we sometimes have a choice among authorities, and we ought to look at this phenomenon within the experiment. It is possible that when different authorities simultaneously call for opposing lines of action, a person's own values will prevail and determine which authority he follows. Or perhaps the net outcome will be a compromise between the two conflicting authorities. Conceivably, this situation will lead to heightened conflict in the subject, who must decide not only whether or not to shock the victim but also which authority to follow. We may also learn something of the circumstances under which the effective exercise of authority is possible, and when it is not.

Experiment 15:
Two Authorities: Contradictory Commands

In this variation when the subject arrived at the laboratory he was confronted with two experimenters, each clad in a grey technician's coat, who alternated in reciting the instructions. The two experimenters were of approximately the same age and height, but one (Experimenter I) gave the appearance of being slightly softer in manner than the other (Experimenter II). The usual victim – our rotund accountant – served in this

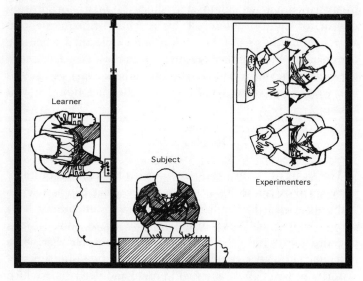

Fig 16 Two authorities: contradictory commands

experiment and was duly strapped into his chair. Everything proceeded as in the standard condition. Both experimenters were seated behind their control table, and both appeared active in recording responses. Their seeming accord came to an abrupt end at the 150–volt level. (It is to be recalled that it is at this point that the victim emits his first truly vehement protest.) One experimenter gives the usual command to proceed with the experiment. However, the second experimenter indicates precisely the opposite, directing his remark at the naïve subject.

The pressure applied by the malevolent authority is no less

than that in other conditions. He prods the subject to continue, indicating that he has no other choice in the matter. But the thrust of his command is undercut by the second authority, who proclaims exactly the opposite.

The net effect was less strained than we might have expected. The experimenters appeared as two bosses who disagreed and were equally convinced of the correctness of their respective positions. Rather than arguing with each other, however, the experimenters focused their remarks on the subject. The subject thus found himself confronted with conflicting and equally authoritative commands. Here is a sample transcript of their exchange:

EXPERIMENTER I: We'll have to stop.

EXPERIMENTER II: The experiment requires that we go on. Please continue, teacher.

SUBJECT: Oh boy.

EXPERIMENTER I: The subject is in pain. We cannot go on with the experiment.

EXPERIMENTER II: We have no other choice gentlemen; the experiment requires that we go on. Please continue.

EXPERIMENTER I: Stop! We're not to go on with the experiment.

EXPERIMENTER II: Mr Williams, the experiment requires that we go on.

SUBJECT: I wish you two would make up your minds.
[Pause.]

SUBJECT: Wait, wait. Which is it going to be? One says stop, one says go. Which one is it?

The subject is confronted with two incompatible prescriptions for action, each issued by an authoritative figure. The outcome of the experiment is shown in Table 4 and is unequivocal. Of 20 subjects, one broke off before the disagreement and 18 stopped at precisely the point where the disagreement between the authorities first occurred. Another broke off one step beyond this point. It is clear that the disagreement between the authorities completely paralysed action. Not a single subject 'took advantage' of the instructions to go on; in no instance did individual aggressive motives latch on to the authoritative sanction provided by the malevolent authority. Rather, action was stopped dead in its tracks.

It is important to note, in contrast, that in other variations nothing the victim did – no pleas, screams, or any other response to the shocks – produced an effect as abrupt and unequivocal. The reason is that action flows from the higher end of a social hierarchy to the lower; that is, the subject is responsive to signals from a level above his own, but indifferent to those below it. Once the signal emanating from the higher level was 'contaminated', the coherence of the hierarchical system was destroyed, along with its efficacy in regulating behaviour.

An interesting phenomenon emerged in this experiment. Some subjects attempted repeatedly to reconstruct a meaningful hierarchy. Their efforts took the form of trying to ascertain which of the two experimenters was the higher authority. There is a certain discomfort in not knowing who the boss is, and subjects sometimes frantically sought to determine this.

Experiment 16:
Two Authorities: One as Victim

In the variation just described, every effort was made to equalise the apparent authority of the two experimenters, by selecting identical garb and equal seating positions and by apportioning the experimental instructions equally to each of them. Thus not merely the status of each but also the position of each within the structure of the situation was made to appear as identical as possible. Yet there is an interesting question raised by this experiment. Is it merely the fiat designation of authority or is it the equality of position in concrete terms that accounts for the experimental effects? That is, does authority reside merely in the designation of rank or is it in significant degree dependent upon the actual position of the individual within the structure of action in the situation? Consider, for example, that a king may possess enormous authority while on his throne, yet not be able to command when cast into prison. The basis of his power resides in part in his actual functioning as an authority, with all its accoutrements. Moreover, given the fact that conflicting multiple authorities cannot jointly occupy a similar locus in a hierarchical structure, situational advantages accruing to one or another of the conflicting authorities may be sufficient to shift allegiance to him. Let us leave this somewhat speculative discussion and go on to an experimental examination of this issue.

This variation is similar in general design to the one

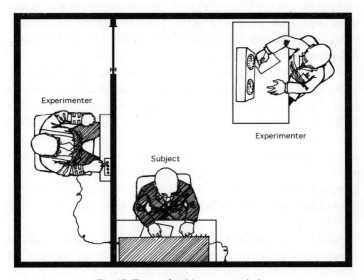

Fig. 17 Two authorities: one as victim

described above, in that the subject confronts two experimenters, alike in appearance and apparent authority. However, at the outset, while the two experimenters and the subject are waiting for the fourth participant to appear, a phone call is received in the laboratory. The fourth participant, it appears, has cancelled his appointment. The experimenters express disappointment, indicating that they have a particular need to complete the accumulation of data that night. One suggests that an experimenter might serve as a subject – that, though a poor substitute, he would at least enable them to meet their experimental quota. The experimenters flip a coin to determine which one will serve in this way. The loser then draws with the subject to determine who will be teacher and who learner. The rigged drawing makes the experimenter the learner, and he is strapped into the chair. He performs like the regular victim. Thus, at 150 volts he shouts that he has had enough and demands to be let out of the experiment. However, the second experimenter insists that the experiment continue. Here there is an important difference from the previous double-authority experiment: the two authorities issuing contradictory commands are no longer in symmetrical positions within the structure of the situation. One has been defined into the victim's role, and the other has been defined, by the flip of a coin, into the superordinate status.

The results of this experiment are shown in Table 4.

What occurs is quite striking: the experimenter, strapped into the electric chair, fares no better than a victim who is not an authority at all. True, virtually all subjects either break off completely when he demands to be let out or completely disregard him. Every score save one falls into this all-or-none pattern. But in total he is no better treated than an ordinary person in the same situation. Apparently, he has lost whatever power he possessed as an authority. Consider, then, the following three results:

1. When an ordinary man gave the order to shock an experimenter, not a single person carried out the order after the experimenter's first protest (Experiment 14).

2. When two experimenters of equal status, both seated at the command desk, gave incompatible orders, no shocks were delivered at all (Experiment 15).

3. When an experimenter commanded a subject to administer shocks to his colleague, the colleague's protests had no more effect than those of an ordinary person (Experiment 16).

The first question is, Why did the experimenter, placed in the role of victim, lose his authority in this situation, while he did not in Experiment 15?

The most pervasive principle is that the subject's action is directed by the person of higher status. Simultaneously there is pressure to find a coherent line of action in this situation. Such a line becomes evident only when there is a clear hierarchy lacking contradictions and incompatible elements.

Comparison with Experiment 14

In Experiment 14, in breaking off at the experimenter's first protest, the subject observed the principle that action is controlled by the individual possessing higher status. Mr March's effort to force shocks on the experimenter was a fiasco. As soon as the experimenter demanded that he be let out, all subjects did so. In no sense did Mr March's countermanding orders constitute serious competition. He lacked the status to be taken seriously and appeared as a child who attempts to command the army by jumping into the general's boots. Inevitably, action was controlled by the person of higher authority.

Comparison with Experiment 15

In Experiment 15, when two experimenters gave contradictory commands from the command desk, all action was paralysed, for there was no clearly discernible higher authority, and consequently no means to determine what line of action to follow. It is the essence of a viable authority system that an individual takes orders from a higher source and executes them toward a stipulated object. The minimum conditions for the operation of this system are an intelligible and coherent command. When there are contradictory commands, the subject finds out who is the boss and acts accordingly. When there is no basis for a decision on this matter, action cannot proceed. The command is incoherent at its source. The circuitry of authority must be free of such contradictions if it is to be effective.

Why does one experimenter fully lose his authority in Experiment 16? Subjects are predisposed to perceive clear hierarchies lacking contradictions and incompatible elements.

They will, therefore, use whatever bases are possible to ascertain and respond to the higher authority. Within the situation:

1. One experimenter has willingly assumed the role of victim. Thus he has temporarily diminished his commanding status, vis-à-vis the other experimenter.

2. Authority is not a mere fiat designation but the occupancy of a particular locus of action within a socially defined occasion. The king in the dungeon finds that the compliance he could elicit from his throne has evaporated. The ex-experimenter finds himself in the physical situation of the victim and confronting an authority seated in the command chair.

3. This is sufficient to give an edge in perceived authority to the experimenter at the control desk, and this slight increment is critical. For it is in the nature of hierarchical control that the response is linked in all-or-none fashion to the person of highest status. It need not be a great deal more status; a smidgen will do. Like the addition of a pebble to a balanced seesaw, control is fully determined in all-or-none fashion by a small increment. The net effect is not a compromise.

Authority systems must be based on people arranged in a hierarchy. Thus the critical question in determining control is, Who is over whom? How much over is far less important than the visible presence of a ranked ordering.

CHAPTER 9

GROUP EFFECTS

The individual is weak in his solitary opposition to authority, but the group is strong. The archetypic event is depicted by Freud (1921), who recounts how oppressed sons band together and rebel against the despotic father. Delacroix portrays the mass in revolt against unjust authority; Gandhi successfully pits the populace against British authority in nonviolent encounter; prisoners at Attica Penitentiary organise and temporarily challenge prison authority. The individual's relationship with his peers can compete with, and on occasion supplant, his ties to authority.

Distinction Between Conformity and Obedience

At this point a distinction must be made between the terms *obedience* and *conformity*. *Conformity*, in particular, has a very broad meaning, but for the purposes of this discussion, I shall limit it to the action of a subject when he goes along with his peers, people of his own status, who have no special right to direct his behaviour. *Obedience* will be restricted to the action of the subject who complies with authority. Consider a recruit who enters military service. He scrupulously carries out the orders of his superiors. At the same time, he adopts the habits, routines, and language of his peers. The former represents obedience and the latter, conformity.

A series of brilliant experiments on conformity has been carried out by S. E. Asch (1951). A group of six apparent subjects was shown a line of a certain length and asked to say which of three other lines matched it. All but one of the subjects in the group had been secretly instructed beforehand to select one of the 'wrong' lines on each trial or in a certain percentage of the trials. The naïve subject was so placed that he heard the answers of most of the group before he had to announce his own decision. Asch found that under this form of social pressure a large fraction of subjects went along with the group rather than accept the unmistakable evidence of their own eyes.

Asch's subjects *conform* to the group. The subjects in the present experiment *obey* the experimenter. Obedience and conformity both refer to the abdication of initiative to an external source. But they differ in the following important ways:

1. *Hierarchy*. Obedience to authority occurs within a hierarchical structure in which the actor feels that the person above has the right to prescribe behaviour. Conformity regulates the behaviour among those of equal status; obedience links one status to another.

2. *Imitation*. Conformity is imitation but obedience is not. Conformity leads to homogenisation of behaviour, as the influenced person comes to adopt the behaviour of peers. In obedience, there is compliance without imitation of the influencing source. A soldier does not simply repeat an order given to him but carries it out.

3. *Explicitness*. In obedience, the prescription for action is explicit, taking the form of an order or command. In conformity, the requirement of going along with the group often remains implicit. Thus, in Asch's experiment on group pressure, there is no overt requirement made by group members that the subject go along with them. The action is spontaneously adopted by the subject. Indeed, many subjects would resist an explicit demand by group members to conform, for the situation is defined as one consisting of equals who have no right to order each other about.

4. *Voluntarism*. The clearest distinction between obedience and conformity, however, occurs after the fact – that is, in the manner in which subjects explain their behaviour. Subjects *deny* conformity and *embrace* obedience as the explanation of their actions. Let me clarify this. In Asch's experiments on group pressure, subjects typically understate the degree to which their actions were influenced by members of the group. They belittle

the group effect and try to play up their own autonomy, even when they have yielded to the group on every trial. They often insist that if they made errors in judgment, these were nonetheless their own errors, attributable to their faulty vision or bad judgment. They minimise the degree to which they have conformed to the group.

In the obedience experiment, the reaction is diametrically opposite. Here the subject explains his action of shocking the victim by denying any personal involvement and attributing his behaviour exclusively to an external requirement imposed by authority. Thus, while the conforming subject insists that his autonomy was not impaired by the group, the obedient subject asserts that he had no autonomy in the matter of shocking the victim and that his actions were completely out of his own hands.

Why is this so? Because conformity is a response to pressures that are implicit, the subject interprets his own behaviour as voluntary. He cannot pinpoint a legitimate reason for yielding to his peers, so he denies that he has done so, not only to the experimenter but to himself as well. In obedience the opposite is true. The situation is publicly defined as one devoid of voluntarism, for there is an explicit command that he is expected to obey. The subject falls back on this public definition of the situation as the full explanation of his action.

So the psychological effects of obedience and conformity are different. Both are powerful forms of social influence, and we may now investigate their role in this experiment.[9]

Experiment 17: Two Peers Rebel

We have said that the revolt against malevolent authority is most effectively brought about by collective rather than individual action. This is a lesson that every revolutionary group learns, and it can be demonstrated in the laboratory with a simple experiment. We have previously seen that there is a marked discrepancy between the subjects' moral principles and their actual performance in the laboratory. Despite their protests and obvious conflict in shocking the victim, a substantial number of subjects are unable to defy the experimenter's authority, and they proceed to administer the highest shock levels commanded by him.

We may now examine in what degree group influence can release the subject from authoritarian control and allow him to act in a direction congruent with his values and personal standards. The strategy is to replicate the basic experiment, but with this difference: the subject is placed in the midst of two peers who defy the experimenter and refuse to punish the victim against his will. In what degree will the pressure created by their actions affect the naïve subject's behaviour?

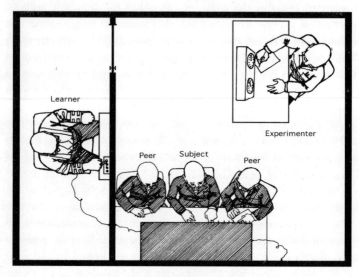

Fig. 18 Two peers rebel

Technique

Four apparent subjects appear at the laboratory to take part in an experiment on the 'effects of collective teaching and punishment on memory and learning'. Three of them are confederates of the experimenter and one is a naïve subject. The experimenter explains that three teachers and one learner are to be used in the study, and by means of a rigged drawing, the naïve subject is assigned the position of teacher 3. The roles of teacher 1, teacher 2, and learner are filled by the confederates. The learner is strapped into the electric chair and the three teachers are seated before the shock generator. Teacher 1 is told to read the list of word pairs, teacher 2 tells the subject whether his answer is correct or incorrect, and teacher 3 (the naïve subject) administers punishment. As in the basic experiment, the subjects are instructed to raise the shock level one step each time the learner makes an error.

Behaviour of confederates. The confederates comply with the experimenter's orders through the 150-volt shock, which provokes the victim's first vehement protest. At this point teacher 1 informs the experimenter that he does not wish to participate further, because of the learner's complaints. The experimenter insists that teacher 1 continue. However, teacher 1 is not swayed by the experimenter's commands, gets up from his chair in front of the shock generator, and takes a seat in another part of the room. Since the experimenter's efforts to get the subject to return to the generator are futile, the experimenter instructs the remaining two subjects to continue with the experiment. Teacher 3 (the naïve subject) is to handle the reading of word pairs, in addition to his regular job of administering electric shock to the learner.

After shock level 14 (210 volts) is administered, teacher 2, expressing concern for the learner, refuses to participate further. The experimenter orders him to continue, but he too leaves his chair in front of the generator and seats himself at an opposite corner of the room, saying, 'I'm willing to answer any of your questions, but I'm not willing to shock that man against his will. I'll have no part of it.'

At this point the naïve subject is seated alone in front of the shock generator. He has witnessed the defiant actions of two peers. The experimenter orders him to continue, stating that it is essential that the experiment be completed.

The results of the experiment are shown in Table 5. In this group setting, 36 of the 40 subjects defy the experimenter (while the corresponding number in the absence of group pressure is 14). The effects of peer rebellion are very impressive in undercutting the experimenter's authority. Indeed, of the score of experimental variations completed in this study, none was so effective in undercutting the experimenter's authority as the manipulation reported here.

Reactions to the defiant peers. The reactions of naïve subjects to the defiant confederates varied considerably and were in part dependent on the exact point where the subject himself defied the experimenter. A subject who quit simultaneously with the first confederate stated, 'Well, I was already thinking about quitting when the guy broke off.' Most defiant subjects praised the confederates with such statements as, 'I thought they were men of good character, yes I do. When the victim said "Stop", they stopped' (broke off at shock level 11). 'I think they were very sympathetic people . . . and they were totally unaware of what was in store for them' (broke off at shock level 14).

A subject who defied the experimenter at level 21 qualified his approval: 'Well, I think they should continue a little further, but I don't blame them for backing out when they did.'

Four defiant subjects definitely acknowledged the importance of the confederates' actions to their own defiance: 'The thought of stopping didn't enter my mind until it was put there by the other two' (broke off at shock level 14). 'The reason I quit was that I did not wish to seem callous and cruel in the eyes of the other two men who had already refused to go on with the experiment' (broke off at shock level 14). A majority of defiant subjects, however, denied that the confederates' action was the critical factor in their own defiance.

A closer analysis of the experimental situation points to several factors that contribute to the group's effectiveness:

1. The peers instill in the subject the *idea* of defying the experimenter. It may not have occurred to some subjects as a possibility.

2. The lone subject in previous experiments had no way of knowing whether, if he defies the experimenter, he is performing in a bizarre manner or whether this action is a common occurrence in the laboratory. The two examples of disobedience he sees suggest that defiance is a natural reaction to the situation.

Table 5. Maximum Shocks Administered in Group Experiments.

Shock level	Verbal designation and voltage level	Experiment 17 Two Peers Rebel (n = 40)	Experiment 18: Peer Administers Shocks (n = 40)
	Slight shock		
1	15		
2	30		
3	45		
4	60		
	Moderate Shock		
5	75		
6	90		
7	105	1	
8	120		
	Strong Shock		
9	135		
10	150	3	1
11	165	4	
12	180	1	1
	Very Strong Shock		
13	195	4	
14	210	12	1
15	225		
16	240		
	Intense Shock		
17	255		
18	270	4	
19	285		
20	300	2	
	Extreme Intensity Shock		
21	315	3	
22	330		
23	345		
24	360	1	
	Danger : Severe Shock		
25	375		
26	390	1	
27	405		
28	420		
	XXX		
29	435		
30	450	4	37
	Mean maximum shock level	16.45	28.65°
	Percentage obedient subjects	10.0%	92.5%°

° See text, p. 123 for meaning of this figure.

3. The reactions of the defiant confederates define the act of shocking the victim as improper. They provide social confirmation for the subject's suspicion that it is wrong to punish a man against his will, even in the context of a psychological experiment.

4. The defiant confederates remain in the laboratory even after withdrawing from the experiment (they have agreed to answer postexperimental questions). Each additional shock administered by the naïve subject then carries with it a measure of social disapproval from the two confederates.

5. As long as the two confederates participate in the experimental procedure, there is a dispersion of responsibility among the group members for shocking the victim. As the confederates withdraw, responsibility becomes focused on the naïve subject.

6. The naïve subject is a witness to two instances of disobedience and observes the *consequences* of defying the experimenter to be minimal.

7. The experimenter's power may be diminished by the very fact of failing to keep the two confederates in line, in accordance with the general rule that every failure of authority to exact compliance to its commands weakens the perceived power of the authority (Homans, 1961).

The fact that groups so effectively undermine the experimenter's power reminds us that individuals act as they do for three principal reasons: they carry certain internalised standards of behaviour; they are acutely responsive to the sanctions that may be applied to them by authority; and finally, they are responsive to the sanctions potentially applicable to them by the group. When an individual wishes to stand in opposition to authority, he does best to find support for his position from others in his group. The mutual support provided by men for each other is the strongest bulwark we have against the excesses of authority. (Not that the group is always on the right side of the issue. Lynch mobs and groups of predatory hoodlums remind us that groups may be vicious in the influence they exert.)

Experiment 18: A Peer Administers Shocks

Authority is not blind to the uses of groups and will ordinarily seek to employ them in a manner that facilitates submission. A simple variation of the experiment demonstrates this possibility. Any force or event that is placed between the subject and the consequences of shocking the victim, any factor that will create distance between the subject and the victim, will lead to a reduction of strain on the participant and thus lessen disobedience. In modern society others often stand between us and the final destructive act to which we contribute.

Indeed, it is typical of modern bureaucracy, even when it is designed for destructive purposes, that most people involved in its organisation do not directly carry out any destructive actions. They shuffle papers or load ammunition or perform some other act which, though it contributes to the final destructive effect, is remote from it in the eyes and mind of the functionary.

To examine this phenomenon within the laboratory, a variation was carried out in which the act of shocking the victim was removed from the naïve subject and placed in the hands of another participant (a confederate). The naïve subject performs subsidiary acts which, though contributing to the overall progress of the experiment, remove him from the actual act of depressing the lever on the shock generator.

And the subject's new role is easy to bear. Table 5 shows the distribution of breakoff points for 40 subjects. Only 3 of the 40 refuse to participate in the experiment to the end. They are accessories to the act of shocking the victim, but they are not psychologically implicated in it to the point where strain arises and disobedience results.

Any competent manager of a destructive bureaucratic system can arrange his personnel so that only the most callous and obtuse are directly involved in violence. The greater part of the personnel can consist of men and women who, by virtue of their distance from the actual acts of brutality, will feel little strain in their performance of supportive functions. They will feel doubly absolved from responsibility. First, legitimate authority has given full warrant for their actions. Second, they have not themselves committed brutal physical acts.

CHAPTER 10

WHY OBEDIENCE? – AN ANALYSIS

We have now seen several hundred participants in the obedience experiment, and we have witnessed a level of obedience to orders that is disturbing. With numbing regularity good people were seen to knuckle under to the demands of authority and perform actions that were callous and severe. Men who are in everyday life responsible and decent were seduced by the trappings of authority, by the control of their perceptions, and by the uncritical acceptance of the experimenter's definition of the situation into performing harsh acts.

We must attempt to grasp the phenomenon in its theoretical aspect and to inquire more deeply into the causes of obedience. Submission to authority is a powerful and prepotent condition in man. Why is this so?

The Survival Value of Hierarchy

Let us begin our analysis by noting that men are not solitary but function within hierarchical structures. In birds, amphibians, and mammals we find dominance structures (Tinbergen, 1953; Marler, 1967), and in human beings, structures of authority mediated by symbols rather than direct contests of physical strength. The formation of hierarchically organised groupings lends enormous advantage to those so organised in coping with dangers of the physical environment, threats posed by competing species, and potential disruption from within. The advantage of a disciplined militia over a tumultuous crowd lies precisely in the organised, coordinated capacity of the military unit brought into play against individuals acting without direction or structure.

An evolutionary bias is implied in this viewpoint; behaviour like any other of man's characteristics, has through successive generations been shaped by the requirements of survival. Behaviours that did not enhance the chances of survival were successively bred out of the organism because they led to the eventual extinction of the groups that displayed them. A tribe in which some of the members were warriors, while others took care of children and still others were hunters, had an enormous advantage over one in which no division of labour occurred. We look around at the civilisations men have built, and realise that only directed, concerted action could have raised the pyramids, formed the societies of Greece, and lifted man from a pitiable creature struggling for survival to technical mastery of the planet.

The advantages of social organisation reach not only outward toward external goals, but inward as well, giving stability and harmony to the relations among group members. By clearly defining the status of each member, it reduces friction to a minimum. When a wolf pack brings down its prey, for example, the dominant wolf enjoys first privileges, followed by the next dominant one, and so on down the line. Each member's acknowledgment of his place in the hierarchy stabilises the pack. The same is true of human groups: internal harmony is ensured when all members accept the status assigned to them. Challenges to the hierarchy, on the other hand, often provoke violence. Thus, a stable social organisation both enhances the group's ability to deal with its environment and by regulating group relationships reduces internal violence.

A potential for obedience is the prerequisite of such social organisation, and because organisation has enormous survival value for any species, such a capacity was bred into the organism through the extended operation of evolutionary processes. I do not intend this as the end point of my argument, but only the beginning, for we will have gotten nowhere if all we can say is that men obey because they have an instinct for it.

Indeed, the idea of a simple instinct for obedience is not what is now proposed. Rather, we are born with a *potential* for obedience, which then interacts with the influence of society to produce the obedient man. In this sense, the capacity for obedience is like the capacity for language: certain highly specific mental structures must be present if the organism is to have potential for language, but exposure to a social milieu is needed to create a speaking man. In explaining the causes of obedience, we need to look both at the inborn structures and at the social influences impinging after birth. The proportion of influence exerted by each is a moot point. From the standpoint of evolutionary survival, all that matters is that we end up with organisms that can function in hierarchies.[10]

The Cybernetic Viewpoint

A clearer understanding will be found, I believe, by considering the problem from a slightly different point of view – namely, that of cybernetics. A jump from evolution to cybernetics may appear at first arbitrary, but those abreast of current scientific developments know that the interpretation of evolutionary processes from a cybernetic viewpoint has been advanced quite brilliantly in recent years (Ashby, 1956; Wiener, 1950). Cybernetics is the science of regulation or control, and the relevant question is, *What changes must occur in the design of an evolving organism as it moves from a capacity for autonomous functioning to a capacity for functioning within an organisation?* Upon analysis certain minimum requirements necessary to this shift become apparent. While these somewhat general principles may seem far removed from the behaviour of participants in the experiment, I am convinced that they are very much at the root of the behaviour in question. For the main question in any scientific theory of obedience is, What changes occur when the autonomously acting individual is embedded in a social structure where he functions as a component of a system rather than on his own? Cybernetic theory, by providing us with a model, can alert us to the changes that logically *must* occur when independent entities are brought into hierarchical functioning. Insofar as human beings participate in such systems, they must be subject to these general laws.

We begin by specifying a design for a simplified creature, or automaton. We will ask, What modifications in its design are required if it is to move from self-regulation to hierarchical functioning? And we will treat the problem not in a historical manner but purely formally.

Consider a set of automata, *a, b, c,* and so on, each designed to function in isolation. Each automaton is characterised as an open system, requiring inputs from the environment to maintain its internal states. The need for environmental inputs (e.g., nourishment) requires apparatus for searching out, ingesting, and converting parts of the environment to usable nutritive forms. Action is initiated via effectors triggered when inner conditions signal a deficiency threatening the automaton's vital states. The signal activates search procedures for nutritive inputs that restore the system to a state of viable functioning.

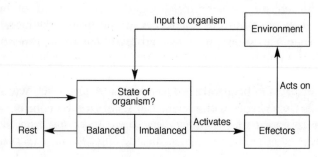

Fig. 19 Simple homeostatic model

Cannon's homeostatic model (1932) points to the ubiquitousness of such state-restoring systems in living organisms.

The automata now dwell apart as self-regulating omnivores. To bring them together, even in the most primitive and undifferentiated form of social organisation, something must be added to the model we have designed. A curb must be placed on the unregulated expression of individual appetites, for unless this is done, mutual destruction of the automata will result. That is, other automata will simply be treated as parts of the environment and destroyed or acted upon for their nutritive value. Therefore a critical new feature must be added to the design: an inhibitor that prevents automata from acting against each other. With the addition of this general inhibitor these automata will be able to occupy the same geographic area without danger of mutual destruction. The greater the degree of mutual dependency among the automata, the more widely ranged and effective these inhibitory mechanisms need to be.

More generally, when action is initiated by tensions originating within the individual, some mechanisms internal to the individual must inhibit that expression, if only to prevent its being directed against kindred members of the species in question. If such an inhibitory mechanism does not evolve, the species perishes, and evolutionary processes must come up with a new design compatible with survival. As Ashby (1956) reminds us:

> The organisms we see today are deeply marked by the selective action of two thousand million years attrition. Any form in any way defective in its power of survival has been eliminated; and today the features of almost every form bear the marks of being adapted to ensure survival rather than any other possible outcome. Eyes, roots, cilia, shells and claws are so fashioned as to maximise the chance of survival. And when we study the brain we are again studying a means to survival. (p. 196)

Is there anything in human beings that corresponds to the inhibitory mechanisms this analysis requires? The question is rhetorical, for we know that the impulse to gratify instincts destructive to others is checked by a part of our nature. Conscience or superego are the terms used to refer to this inhibitory system, and its function is to check the unregulated expression of impulses having their origin in the tensional system of the person. If our automata are beginning to take on some of the properties and structures present in human beings, it is not because human beings provided the model, but rather because parallel design problems arise in constructing any system in which the member organisms sustain themselves through environmental inputs but do not destroy their own kind.

The presence of conscience in men, therefore, can be seen as a special case of the more general principle that any self-regulating automaton must have an inhibitor to check its actions against its own kind, for without such inhibition, several automata cannot occupy a common territory. The inhibitor filters or checks actions that have their origin in internal imbalances of the automaton. In the case of the human organism – if we may employ psychoanalytic terminology – instinctual urges having their origin in the id are not immediately channelled into action but are subjected to the inhibitory checks of the superego. We note that most men, as civilians, will not hurt, maim, or kill others in the normal course of the day.

Hierarchical Structuring

The automata now act individually, limited only by the inhibition against hurting their own kind. What will happen when we try to organise several automata so they function together? The joining of elements to act in a concerted fashion may best be achieved by creating an external source of coordination for two or more elements. Control proceeds from the emitting point to each of the automata.

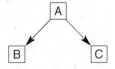

Still more powerful social mechanisms can be achieved by having each subordinate element serve as a superordinate to elements in a level below.

The diagram comes to assume the typical pyramidal form for hierarchical organisation. Yet this organisation cannot be achieved with the automata as we have described them. The internal design of each element must be altered. Control at the level of each local element must be given up in favour of control from a superordinate point. *The inhibitory mechanisms which are vital when the individual element functions by itself become secondary to the need to cede control to the coordinating component.*

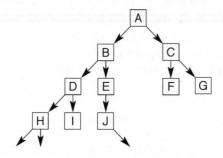

More generally, whenever elements that function autonomously are brought into a system of hierarchical coordination, changes are required in the internal structure of the elements. These changes constitute the system requirements, and they invariably entail some suppression of local control in the interest of system coherence. System coherence is attained when all parts of the system are functioning in harmony and not at cross purposes.

From an evolutionary standpoint each *autonomously* functioning element must be regulated against the unrestrained pursuit of appetites, of which the individual element is the chief beneficiary. The superego, conscience, or some similar mechanism that pits moral ideals against the uncontrolled expression of impulses fulfils this function. However, in the organisational mode, it is crucial for the operation of the system that these inhibitory mechanisms do not significantly conflict with directions from higher-level components. Therefore when the individual is working *on his own*, conscience is brought into play. But when he functions in an organisational mode, directions that come from the higher-level component are not assessed against the internal standards of moral judgment. Only impulses generated within the individual, in the autonomous mode, are so checked and regulated.

The hierarchy is constructed of modules, each consisting of one boss with followers (e.g., A: B,C). Each follower, in turn, may be superior to others below him (e.g., B: D, E), the entire structure being built up of such interlocking units. The psychology of obedience does not depend on the placement of the module within the larger hierarchy: the psychological adjustments of an obedient Wehrmacht General to Adolf Hitler parallel those of the lowest infantryman to his superior, and so forth, throughout the system. Only the psychology of the ultimate leader demands a different set of explanatory principles.

Variability

We now need to make clear a point that has been implicit in the argument – namely, the relationship of variability to the need for systemic modification. Where variability is present, efficient structuring into larger systems can only occur by ceding local control to a coordinating component. If not, the larger system will be less efficient than an average individual unit.

Consider a set of identical entities that can function on their own, say a set of five electric trams that possess governing mechanisms that brake each tram precisely at 50 miles an hour. As long as there is no variability among the individual units, when they are linked together in a five-car train, the train can move along at 50 miles an hour. Consider now that variability is introduced, and the automatic speed governors brake the five cars at 10, 20, 30, 40, and 50 miles an hour respectively. If the cars are formed into a supraordinate system, the train as a whole cannot move faster than the slowest unit.

If a social organisation consists of individuals whose judgments on a course of action vary, coherence can only be secured by relying on the least common denominator. This is the least efficient system possible and hardly likely to benefit its members. Thus suppression of control at the level of the local unit and ceding to higher-level components become ever more important as variability increases. Variability, as evolutionary theorists have long told us, is of enormous biological value. And it is conspicuously a feature of the human species. Because people are not all alike, in order to derive the benefit of hierarchical structuring, readily effected suppression of local control is needed at the point of entering the hierarchy, so that the least efficient unit does not determine the operation of the system as a whole.

It is instructive to list a few of the systems that function by suppression of local control: individual pilots cede control to the controller in the tower as they approach an airport so that the units can be brought into a coordinated landing system; military units cede control to higher-level authority to ensure unity of action. When individuals enter a condition of hierarchical control, the mechanism which ordinarily regulates individual impulses is suppressed and ceded to the higher-level component. Freud (1921), without referring to the general systems implications of his assertion, spelled out this mechanism clearly: '. . . the individual gives up his ego ideal and substitutes for it the group ideal embodied in the leader' (page 78, *Group Psychology*). The basic reason why this occurs is rooted not in individual needs but in organisational needs. Hierarchical structures can function only if they possess the quality of coherence, and coherence can be attained only by the suppression of control at the local level.

Let me summarise the argument so far: (1) organised social life provides survival benefits to the individuals who are part of it, and to the group; (2) whatever behavioural and psychological features have been necessary to produce the capacity for *organised* social life have been shaped by evolutionary forces; (3) from the standpoint of cybernetics, the most general need in bringing self-regulating automata into a coordinated hierarchy is to suppress individual direction and control in favour of control from higher-level components; (4) more generally, hierarchies can function only when internal modification occurs in the elements of which they are composed; (5) functional hierarchies in social life are characterised by each of these features, and (6) the individuals who enter into such hierarchies are, of necessity, modified in their functioning.

This analysis is of importance for one reason alone: it alerts us to the changes that must occur when an independently functioning unit becomes part of a system. This transformation corresponds precisely to the central dilemma of our experiment: how is it that a person who is usually decent and courteous acts with severity against another person within the experiment? He does so because conscience, which regulates impulsive aggressive action, is per force diminished at the point of entering a hierarchical structure.

The Agentic Shift

We have concluded that internal modification is required in the operation of any element that can successfully function in a hierarchy, and that in the case of self-directed automata this entails suppression of local control in favour of regulation by a higher-level component. The design of such an automaton, if it is to parallel human function, must be sufficiently flexible to allow for two modes of operation: the self-directed (or autonomous mode), when it is functioning on its own, and for the satisfaction of its own internal needs, and the systemic mode, when the automaton is integrated into a larger organisational structure. Its behaviour will depend on which of the two states it is in.

Social organisations, and the individuals who participate in them, are not exempt from the requirements of system integration. What in human experience corresponds to the transition from the autonomous to the systemic mode, and what are its consequences in specifically human terms? To answer the question we must move from a general level of discourse to the close examination of a person as he shifts into a functional position in a social hierarchy.

Where in a human being shall we find the switch that controls the transition from an autonomous to a systemic mode? No less than in the case of automata, there is certainly an alteration in the internal operations of the person, and these, no doubt, reduce to shifts in patterns of neural functioning. Chemical inhibitors and disinhibitors alter the probability of certain neural pathways and sequences being used. But it is totally beyond our technical skill to specify this event at the chemoneurological level. However, there is a phenomeno-logical expression of this shift to which we do have access. The critical shift in functioning is reflected in an alteration of attitude. Specifically, the person entering an authority system no longer views himself as acting out of his own purposes but rather comes to see himself as an agent for executing the wishes of another person. Once an individual conceives his action in this light, profound alterations occur in his behaviour and his internal functioning. These are so pronounced that one may say that this altered attitude places the individual in a different state from the one he was in prior to integration into the hierarchy. I shall term this *the agentic state*, by which I mean the condition a person is in when he sees himself as an agent for carrying out another person's wishes. This term will be used in opposition to that of *autonomy* – that is, when a person sees himself as acting on his own.

The agentic state is the master attitude from which the observed behaviour flows. The state of agency is more than a terminological burden imposed on the reader; it is the keystone of our analysis. If it is useful, we shall find that the laboratory observations will hang together when linked by it. If it is superfluous we shall find that it adds nothing to the coherence of our findings. For clarity, let me again define what is meant by the state of agency. It may be defined both from a cybernetic and a phenomenological standpoint.

From the standpoint of cybernetic analysis, the agentic state occurs when a self-regulating entity is internally modified so as to allow its functioning within a system of hierarchical control.

From a subjective standpoint, a person is in a state of agency when he defines himself in a social situation in a manner that renders him open to regulation by a person of higher status. In this condition the individual no longer views himself as responsible for his own actions but defines himself as an instrument for carrying out the wishes of others.

An element of free choice determines whether the person defines himself in this way or not, but given the presence of certain critical releasers, the propensity to do so is exceedingly strong, and the shift is not freely reversible.

Since the agentic state is largely a state of mind, some will say that this shift in attitude is not a *real* alteration in the state of the person. I would argue, however, that these shifts in individuals are precisely equivalent to those major alterations in the logic system of the automata considered earlier. Of course, we do not have toggle switches emerging from our bodies, and the shifts are synaptically effected, but this makes them no less real.

CHAPTER 11

THE PROCESS OF OBEDIENCE:
APPLYING THE ANALYSIS TO THE EXPERIMENT

Now that the agentic state is at the centre of our analysis (diagrammed on next page), certain key questions arise. First, under what conditions will a person move from an autonomous to an agentic state? (antecedent conditions). Second, once the shift has occurred, what behavioural and psychological properties of the person are altered? (consequences). And, third, what keeps a person in the agentic state? (binding factors). Here a distinction is made between the conditions that produce entry into a state and those that maintain it. Let us now consider the process in detail.

Antecedent Conditions of Obedience

First, we need to consider forces that acted on the person before he became our subject, forces that shaped his basic orientation to the social world and laid the groundwork for obedience.

Family

The subject has grown up in the midst of structures of authority. From his very first years, he was exposed to parental regulation, whereby a sense of respect for adult authority was inculcated. Parental injunctions are also the source of moral imperatives. However, when a parent instructs a child to follow a moral injunction, he is, in fact, doing two things. First, he presents a specific ethical content to be followed. Second, he trains the child to comply with authoritative injunctions per se. Thus when a parent says, 'Don't strike smaller children,' he provides not one imperative but two. The first concerns the manner in which the recipient of the command is to treat smaller children (the prototype of those who are helpless and innocent); the second and implicit imperative is, 'And obey me!' Thus, the very genesis of our moral ideals is inseparable from the inculcation of an obedient attitude. Moreover, the demand for obedience remains the only consistent element across a variety of specific commands, and thus tends to acquire a prepotent strength relative to any particular moral content.[11]

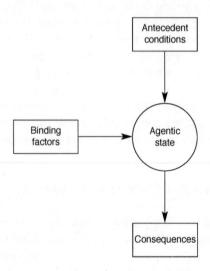

Institutional Setting

As soon as the child emerges from the cocoon of the family, he is transferred to an *institutional system of authority*, the school. Here, the child learns not merely a specific curriculum but also how to function within an organisational framework. His actions are, to a significant degree, regulated by his teachers, but he can perceive that they in turn are subjected to the discipline and requirements of a headmaster. The student observes that arrogance is not passively accepted by authority but severely rebuked and that deference is the only appropriate and comfortable response to authority.

The first twenty years of the young person's life are spent functioning as a subordinate element in an authority system, and upon leaving school, the male usually moves into either a civilian job or military service. On the job, he learns that although some discreetly expressed dissent is allowable, an underlying posture of submission is required for harmonious functioning with superiors. However much freedom of detail is allowed the individual, the situation is defined as one in which he is to do a job prescribed by someone else.

While structures of authority are of necessity present in all societies, advanced or primitive, modern society has the added characteristic of teaching individuals to respond to *impersonal* authorities. Whereas submission to authority is probably no less for an Ashanti than for an American factory worker, the range of persons who constitute authorities for the native are all personally known to him, while the modern industrial world forces individuals to submit to impersonal authorities, so that responses are made to abstract rank, indicated by an insignia, uniform or title.

Rewards

Throughout this experience with authority, there is continual confrontation with a reward structure in which compliance with authority has been generally rewarded, while failure to comply has most frequently been punished. Although many forms of reward are meted out for dutiful compliance, the most ingenious is this: the individual is moved up a niche in the hierarchy, thus both motivating the person and perpetuating the structure simultaneously. This form of reward, 'the promotion', carries with it profound emotional gratification for the individual but its special feature is the fact that it ensures the continuity of the hierarchical form.

The net result of this experience is the *internalisation of the social order* – that is, internalising the set of axioms by which social life is conducted. And the chief axiom is: do what the man in charge says. Just as we internalise grammatical rules, and can thus both understand and produce new sentences, so we internalise axiomatic rules of social life which enable us to fulfil social requirements in novel situations. In any hierarchy of rules, that which requires compliance to authority assumes a paramount position.

Among the antecedent conditions, therefore, are the individual's familial experience, the general societal setting built on impersonal systems of authority, and extended experience with a reward structure in which compliance with authority is rewarded, and failure to comply punished. While without doubt providing the background against which our subject's habits of conduct were formed, these conditions are beyond the control of experimentation and do not immediately trigger movement to the agentic state. Let us now turn to the more immediate factors, within a specific situation, that lead to the agentic state.

Immediate Antecedent Conditions

Perception of authority. The first condition needed for transformation to the agentic state is the perception of a legitimate authority. From a psychological standpoint, authority means the person who is perceived to be in a position of social control within a given situation. Authority is contextually perceived and does not necessarily transcend the situation in which it is encountered. For example, should the experimenter encounter the subject on the street, he would have no special influence on him. A pilot's authority over his passengers does not extend beyond the airplane. Authority is normatively supported: there is a shared expectation among people that certain situations do ordinarily have a socially controlling figure. Authority need not possess high status in the sense of 'prestige'. For example, an usher at a theatre is a source of social control to whom we ordinarily submit willingly. The power of an authority stems not from personal characteristics but from his perceived position in a social structure.

The question of how authority communicates itself seems, at first, not to require a special answer. We invariably seem to know who is in charge. We may, nonetheless, examine the behaviour in the laboratory to try to dissect the process a little.

First, the subject enters the situation with the expectation that *someone* will be in charge. Thus, the experimenter, upon first presenting himself, fills a gap experienced by the subject. Accordingly, the experimenter need not assert his authority, but merely identify it. He does so through a few introductory remarks, and since this self-defining ritual fits perfectly with the subject's expectation of encountering a man in charge, it is not challenged. A supporting factor is the confidence and 'air of authority' exhibited by the experimenter. Just as a servant possesses a deferential manner, so his master exudes a commanding presence that subtly communicates his dominant status within the situation at hand.

Second, external accoutrements are often used to signify the authority in a given situation. Our experimenter was dressed in a grey technician's coat, which linked him to the laboratory. Police, military, and other service uniforms are the most conspicuous signs of authority within common experience. Third, the subject notes the absence of competing authorities. (No one else claims to be in charge, and this helps confirm the presumption that the experimenter is the right man.) Fourth, there is the absence of conspicuously anomalous factors (e.g., a child of five claiming to be the scientist).

It is the appearance of authority and not actual authority to which the subject responds. Unless contradictory information or anomalous facts appear, the self-designation of the authority almost always suffices.[12]

Entry into the Authority System. A second condition triggering the shift to the agentic state is the act of defining the person as part of the authority system in question. It is not enough that we perceive an authority, he must be an authority relevant to us. Thus, if we watch a parade, and hear a Colonel shout, 'Left face', we do not turn left, for we have not been defined as subordinate to his command. There is always a transition from that moment when we stand outside an authority system to that point when we are inside it. Authority systems are frequently limited by a physical context, and often we come under the influence of an authority when we cross the physical threshold into his domain. The fact that this experiment is carried out in a laboratory has a good deal to do with the degree of obedience exacted. There is a feeling that the experimenter 'owns' the space and that the subject must conduct himself fittingly, as if a guest in someone's house. If the experiment were to be carried on outside the laboratory, obedience would drop sharply.[13]

Even more important, for the present experiment, is the fact that entry into the experimenter's realm of authority is voluntary, undertaken through the free will of the participants. The psychological consequence of voluntary entry is that it creates a sense of commitment and obligation which will subsequently play a part in binding the subject to his role.

Were our subjects forcibly introduced to the experiment, they might well yield to authority, but the psychological mechanisms would be quite different from what we have observed. Generally, and wherever possible, society tries to create a sense of voluntary entry into its various institutions. Upon induction into the military, recruits take an oath of allegiance, and volunteers are preferred to inductees. While people will comply with a source of social control under coercion (as when a gun is aimed at them), the nature of obedience under such circumstances is limited to direct surveillance. When the gunman leaves, or when his capacity for sanctions is eliminated, obedience stops. In the case of voluntary obedience to a legitimate authority, the principal sanctions for disobedience come from within the person. They are not dependent upon coercion, but stem from the individual's sense of commitment to his role. In this sense, *there is an internalised basis for his obedience, not merely an external one.*

Coordination of Command with the Function of Authority. Authority is the perceived source of social control within a specific context. The context defines the range of commands considered appropriate to the authority in question. There must, in general, be some intelligible link between the function of the controlling person, and the nature of the commands he issues. The connection need not be very well worked out but need only make sense in the most general way. Thus, in a military situation, a captain may order a subordinate to perform a highly dangerous action, but he may not order the subordinate to embrace his girlfriend. In one case, the order is logically linked to the general function of the military, and in the other case it is not.[14]

In the obedience experiment, the subject acts within the context of a learning experiment and sees the experimenter's commands as meaningfully coordinated to his role. In the context of the laboratory, such commands are felt to be appropriate in a general way, however much one may argue with certain specific developments that later occur.

Because the experimenter issues orders in a context he is presumed to know something about, his power is increased. Generally, authorities are felt to know more than the person they are commanding; whether they do or not, the occasion is defined as if they do. Even when a subordinate possesses a greater degree of technical knowledge than his superior, he must not presume to override the authority's right to command but must present this knowledge to the superior to dispose of as he wishes. A typical source of strain occurs in authority systems when the person in authority is incompetent to the point of endangering the subordinates.[15]

The Overarching Ideology. The perception of a legitimate source of social control within a defined social occasion is a necessary prerequisite for a shift to the agentic state. But the legitimacy of the occasion itself depends on its articulation to a justifying ideology. When subjects enter the laboratory and are told to perform, they do not in a bewildered fashion cry out, 'I never heard of science. What do you mean by this?' Within this situation, the idea of science and its acceptance as a legitimate social enterprise provide the overarching ideological justification for the experiment. Such institutions as business, the church, the government, and the educational establishment provide other legitimate realms of activity, each justified by the values and needs of society, and also, from the standpoint of the typical person, accepted because they exist as part of the world in which he is born and grows up. Obedience could be secured outside such institutions, but it would not be the form of willing obedience, in which the person complies with a strong sense of doing the right thing. Moreover, if the experiment were carried out in a culture very different from our own – say, among Trobrianders – it would be necessary to find the functional equivalent of science in order to obtain psychologically comparable results. The Trobriander may not believe in scientists, but he respects witch doctors. The inquisitor of sixteenth-century Spain might have eschewed science, but he embraced the ideology of his church, and in its name, and for its preservation, tightened the screw on the rack without any problem of conscience.

Ideological justification is vital in obtaining *willing* obedience, for it permits the person to see his behaviour as serving a desirable end. Only when viewed in this light, is compliance easily exacted.

An authority system, then, consists of a minimum of two persons sharing the expectation that one of them has the right to prescribe behaviour for the other. In the current study, the experimenter is the key element in a system that extends beyond his person. The system includes the setting of the experiment, the impressive laboratory equipment, the devices which inculcate a sense of obligation in the subject, the mystique of science of which the experiment is a part, and the broad institutional accords that permit such activities to go on – that is, the diffuse societal support that is implied by the very fact that the experiment is being run and tolerated in a civilised city.

The experimenter acquires his capacity to influence behaviour not by virtue of the exercise of force or threat but by virtue of the position he occupies in a social structure. There is general agreement not only that he *can* influence behaviour but that he *ought* to be able to. Thus, his power comes about in some degree through the consent of those over whom he presides. But once this consent is initially granted, its withdrawal does not proceed automatically or without great cost.

The Agentic State

What are the properties of the agentic state, and its consequences for the subject?

Moved into the agentic state, the person becomes something different from his former self, with new properties not easily traced to his usual personality.

First, the entire set of activities carried out by the subject comes to be pervaded by his relationship to the experimenter; the subject typically wishes to perform competently and to make a good appearance before this central figure. He directs his attention to those features of the situation required for such competent performance. He attends to the instructions, concentrates on the technical requirements of administering shocks, and finds himself absorbed in the narrow technical tasks at hand. Punishment of the learner shrinks to an insignificant part of the total experience, a mere gloss on the complex activities of the laboratory.

Tuning

Those not familiar with the experiment may think that the predicament of the subject is one in which he is assaulted by conflicting forces emanating from the learner and the experimenter. In a very real sense, however, a process of tuning occurs in the subject, with maximal receptivity to the emissions of the authority, whereas the learner's signals are muted and psychologically remote. Those who are sceptical of this effect might observe the behaviour of individuals organised in a hierarchical structure. The meeting of a company president with his subordinates will do. The subordinates respond with attentive concern to each word uttered by the president. Ideas originally mentioned by persons of a low status will frequently not be heard, but when repeated by the president, they are greeted with enthusiasm.

There is nothing especially malicious in this; it reflects the natural responses to authority. If we explore a little more deeply, we will see why this is so: the person in authority, by virtue of that position, is in the optimal position to bestow benefits or inflict deprivations. The boss can fire or promote; the military superior can send a man into dangerous combat or give him a soft job; the tribal patriarch consents to a marriage or orders an execution; thus, it is highly adaptive to attend with meticulous concern to authority's whim.

Because of this, authority tends to be seen as something larger than the individual. The individual often views authority as an impersonal force, whose dictates transcend mere human wish or desire. Those in authority acquire, for some, a suprahuman character.

The phenomenon of differential tuning occurs with impressive regularity in the experiment at hand. The learner operates under the handicap that the subject is not truly attuned to him, for the subject's feelings and percepts are dominated by the presence of the experimenter. For many subjects, the learner becomes simply an unpleasant obstacle interfering with attainment of a satisfying relationship with the experimenter. His pleas for mercy are consequential only in that they add a certain discomfort to what evidently is required of the subject if he is to gain the approval of the central emotional figure in the situation.

Redefining the Meaning of the Situation

Control the manner in which a man interprets his world, and you have gone a long way toward controlling his behaviour. That is why ideology, an attempt to interpret the condition of man, is always a prominent feature of revolutions, wars, and other circumstances in which individuals are called upon to perform extraordinary action. Governments invest heavily in propaganda, which constitutes the official manner of interpreting events.

Every situation also possesses a kind of ideology, which we call the 'definition of the situation', and which is the interpretation of the meaning of a social occasion. It provides the perspective through which the elements of a situation gain coherence. An act viewed in one perspective may seem heinous;

the same action viewed in another perspective seems fully warranted. *There is a propensity for people to accept definitions of action provided by legitimate authority.* That is, although the subject performs the action, he allows authority to define its meaning.

It is this ideological abrogation to the authority that constitutes the principal cognitive basis of obedience. If, after all, the world or the situation is as the authority defines it, a certain set of actions follows logically.

The relationship between authority and subject, therefore, cannot be viewed as one in which a coercive figure forces action from an unwilling subordinate. Because the subject accepts authority's definition of the situation, action follows willingly.

Loss of Responsibility

The most far-reaching consequence of the agentic shift is that a man feels responsible *to* the authority directing him but feels no responsibility *for* the content of the actions that the authority prescribes. Morality does not disappear, but acquires a radically different focus: the subordinate person feels shame or pride depending on how adequately he has performed the actions called for by authority.

Language provides numerous terms to pinpoint this type of morality: *loyalty, duty, discipline*, all are terms heavily saturated with moral meaning and refer to the degree to which a person fulfils his obligations to authority. They refer not to the 'goodness' of the person per se but to the adequacy with which a subordinate fulfils his socially defined role. The most frequent defence of the individual who has performed a heinous act under command of authority is that he has simply done his duty. In asserting this defence, the individual is not introducing an alibi concocted for the moment but is reporting honestly on the psychological attitude induced by submission to authority.

For a man to feel responsible for his actions, he must sense that the behaviour has flowed from 'the self'. In the situation we have studied, subjects have precisely the opposite view of their actions – namely, they see them as originating in the motives of some other person. Subjects in the experiment frequently said, 'If it were up to me, I would not have administered shocks to the learner.'

Superego functions shift from an evaluation of the goodness or badness of the acts to an assessment of how well or poorly one is functioning in the authority system.[16] Because the inhibitory forces which prevent the individual from acting harshly against others on his own are short-circuited, actions are no longer limited by conscience.

Consider an individual who, in everyday life, is gentle and kind. Even in moments of anger he does not strike out against those who have frustrated him. Feeling that he must spank a mischievous child, he finds the task distasteful; indeed, the very musculature in his arms becomes paralysed, and he abandons the task. Yet, when taken into military service he is ordered to drop bombs on people, and he does so. The act does not originate in his own motive system and thus is not checked by the inhibitory forces of his internal psychological system. In growing up, the normal individual has learned to check the expression of aggressive impulses. But the culture has failed, almost entirely, in inculcating internal controls on actions that have their origin in authority. For this reason, the latter constitutes a far greater danger to human survival.[17]

Self-Image

It is not only important to people that they look good to others, they must also look good to themselves. A person's ego ideal can be an important source of internal inhibitory regulation. Tempted to perform harsh action, he may assess its consequences for his self-image and refrain. But once the person has moved into the agentic state, this evaluative mechanism is wholly absent. The action, since it no longer stems from motives of his own, no longer reflects on his self-image and thus has no consequences for self-conception. Indeed, the individual frequently discerns an opposition between what he himself wishes on the one hand and what is required of him on the other. He sees the action, even though he performs it, as alien to his nature. For this reason, actions performed under command are, from the subject's viewpoint, virtually guiltless, however inhumane they may be. And it is toward authority that the subject turns for confirmation of his worth.

Commands and the Agentic State

The agentic state constitutes a potential out of which specific acts of obedience flow. But something more than the potential is required – namely, specific commands that serve as the triggering mechanism. We have already pointed out that, in a general way, the commands given must be consistent with the role of authority. A command consists of two main parts: a definition of action and the imperative that the action be executed. (A request, for example, contains a definition of action but lacks the insistence that it be carried out.)

Commands, then, lead to specific acts of obedience. Is the agentic state just another word for obedience? No, it is that state of mental organisation which enhances the likelihood of obedience. Obedience is the behavioural aspect of the state. A person may be in an agentic state – that is, in a state of openness to regulation from an authority – without ever being given a command and thus never having to obey.

Binding Factors

Once a person has entered the agentic state, what keeps him in it? Whenever elements are linked in a hierarchy, there need to be forces to maintain them in that relationship. If these did not exist the mildest perturbation would bring about the disintegration of the structure. Therefore, once people are brought into a social hierarchy, there must be some cementing mechanism to endow the structure with at least minimal stability.

Some people interpret the experimental situation as one in which the subject, in a highly rational manner, can weigh the conflicting values in the situation, process the factors according to some mental calculus, and base his actions on the outcome of this equation. Thus, the subject's predicament is reduced to a problem of rational decision making. This analysis ignores a crucial aspect of behaviour illuminated by the experiments. Though many subjects make the intellectual decision that they should not give any more shocks to the learner, they are frequently unable to transform this conviction into action. Viewing these subjects in the laboratory, one can sense their intense inner struggle to extricate themselves from the authority, while ill-defined but powerful bonds hold them at the shock generator. One subject tells the experimenter: 'He can't stand it. I'm not going to kill that man in there. You hear him hollering in there. He's hollering. He can't stand it.' Although at the verbal level the subject has resolved not to go on, he continues to act in accord with the experimenter's commands. Many subjects make tentative movements toward disobedience but then seem restrained, as if by a bond. Let us now examine the forces that powerfully bind a subject to his role.

The best way to begin tracing these forces is to ask: What does the subject have to go through if he wants to break off? Through what psychological underbrush must he cut to get from his position in front of the shock generator to a stance of defiance?

Sequential Nature of the Action

The laboratory hour is an unfolding process in which each action influences the next. The obedient act is perseverative; after the initial instructions, the experimenter does not command the subject to initiate a new act but simply to continue doing what he is doing. The recurrent nature of the action demanded of the subject itself creates binding forces. As the subject delivers more and more painful shocks, he must seek to justify to himself what he has done; one form of justification is to go to the end. For if he breaks off, he must say to himself: 'Everything I have done to this point is bad, and I now acknowledge it by breaking off.' But, if he goes on, he is reassured about his past performance. Earlier actions give rise to discomforts, which are neutralised by later ones.[18] And the subject is implicated into the destructive behaviour in piecemeal fashion.

Situational Obligations

Underlying all social occasions is a situational etiquette that plays a part in regulating behaviour. In order to break off the experiment, the subject must breach the implicit set of understandings that are part of the social occasion. He made an initial promise to aid the experimenter, and now he must renege on this commitment. Although to the outsider the act of refusing to shock stems from moral considerations, the action is experienced by the subject as renouncing an obligation to the experimenter, and such repudiation is not undertaken lightly. There is another side to this matter.

Goffman (1959) points out that every social situation is built upon a working consensus among the participants. One of its chief premises is that once a definition of the situation has been projected and agreed upon by participants, there shall be no challenge to it. Indeed, disruption of the accepted definition by one participant has the character of moral transgression. Under no circumstance is open conflict about the definition of the situation compatible with polite social exchange.

More specifically, according to Goffman's analysis, 'society is organised on the principle that any individual who possesses certain social characteristics has a moral right to expect that others will value and treat him in a correspondingly appropriate way. ... When an individual projects a definition of the situation and then makes an implicit or explicit claim to be a person of a particular kind, he automatically exerts a moral demand upon the others, obliging them to value and treat him in the manner that persons of his kind have a right to expect' (page 185). Since to refuse to obey the experimenter is to reject his claim to competence and authority in this situation, a severe social impropriety is necessarily involved.

The experimental situation is so constructed that there is no way the subject can stop shocking the learner without violating the experimenter's self-definition. The teacher cannot break off and at the same time protect the authority's definitions of his own competence. Thus, the subject fears that if he breaks off, he will appear arrogant, untoward, and rude. Such emotions, although they appear small in scope alongside the violence being done to the learner, nonetheless help bind the subject into obedience. They suffuse the mind and feelings of the subject, who is miserable at the prospect of having to repudiate the authority to his face. The entire prospect of turning against the experimental authority, with its attendant disruption of a well-defined social situation, is an embarrassment that many people are unable to face up to.[19] In an effort to avoid this awkward event, many subjects find obedience a less painful alternative.

In ordinary social encounters precautions are frequently taken to prevent just such disruption of the occasion, but the subject finds himself in a situation where even the discreet exercise of tact cannot save the experimenter from being discredited. Only obedience can preserve the experimenter's status and dignity. It is a curious thing that a measure of compassion on the part of the subject, an unwillingness to 'hurt' the experimenter's feelings, are part of those binding forces inhibiting disobedience. The withdrawal of such deference may be as painful to the subject as to the authority he defies. Readers who feel this to be a trivial consideration ought to carry out the following experiment. It will help them feel the force of inhibition that operates on the subject.

First, identify a person for whom you have genuine respect, preferably someone older than yourself by at least a generation, and who represents an authority in an important life domain. He could be a respected professor, a beloved priest, or under certain circumstances a parent. It must also be a person whom you refer to with some title such as Professor Parsons, Father Paul, or Dr Charles Brown. He must be a person who represents to you the distance and solemnity of a genuine authority. To understand what it means to breach the etiquette of relations with authority, you need merely present yourself to the person and, in place of using his title, whether it be Dr, Professor, or Father, address him using his first name, or perhaps even an appropriate nickname. You may state to Dr Brown, for example, 'Good morning, Charlie!'

As you approach him you will experience anxiety and a powerful inhibition that may well prevent successful completion of the experiment. You may say to yourself: 'Why should I carry out this foolish experiment? I have always had a fine relationship with Dr Brown, which may now be jeopardised. Why should I appear arrogant to him?'

More than likely, you will not be able to perform the disrespectful action, but even in attempting it you will gain a greater understanding of the feelings experienced by our subjects.

Social occasions, the very elements out of which society is built, are held together, therefore, by the operation of a certain situational etiquette, whereby each person respects the definition of the situation presented by another and in this way avoids conflict, embarrassment, and awkward disruption of social exchange. The most basic aspect of that etiquette does not concern the content of what transpires from one person to the next but rather the maintenance of the structural relations between them. Such relations can be those of equality or of hierarchy. When the occasion is defined as one of hierarchy, any attempt to alter the defined structure will be experienced as a moral transgression and will evoke anxiety, shame, embarrassment, and diminished feelings of self-worth.[20, 21]

Anxiety

The fears experienced by the subject are largely anticipatory in nature, referring to vague apprehensions of the unknown. Such diffuse apprehension is termed *anxiety*.

What is the source of this anxiety? It stems from the individual's long history of socialisation. He has, in the course of moving from a biological creature to a civilised person, internalised the basic rules of social life. And the most basic of these is respect for authority. The rules are internally enforced by linking their possible breach to a flow of disruptive, ego-threatening affect. The emotional signs observed in the laboratory – trembling, anxious laughter, acute embarrassment – are evidence of an assault on these rules. As the subject contemplates this break, anxiety is generated, signalling him to step back from the forbidden action and thereby creating an emotional barrier through which he must pass in order to defy authority.

The remarkable thing is, once the 'ice is broken' through disobedience, virtually all the tension, anxiety, and fear evaporate.

CHAPTER 12

STRAIN AND DISOBEDIENCE

Subjects disobey. Why? At first we are inclined to say that they do so because it is immoral to shock the victim. Yet an explanation in terms of moral judgment is not adequate. The morality of shocking a helpless victim remains constant whether the victim is far or near, but we have seen that a simple change in spatial relations substantially alters the proportion of people who disobey. Rather, it is a more general form of strain that propels the subject to disobedience, and we need to understand what strain means, both from a human standpoint and in terms of the theoretical model that has guided our analysis.

Theoretically, strain is likely to arise whenever an entity that can function autonomously is brought into a hierarchy, because the design requirements of an autonomous unit are quite different from those of a component specifically and uniquely designed for systemic functioning. Men can function on their own or, through the assumption of roles, merge into larger systems. But the very fact of dual capacities requires a design compromise. We are not perfectly tailored for complete autonomy, nor for total submission.

Of course, any sophisticated entity designed to function both autonomously and within hierarchical systems will have mechanisms for the resolution of strain, for unless such resolving mechanisms exist the system is bound to break down posthaste. So we shall add one final concept to our model, representing the resolution of strain. And we shall allow ourselves a brief formula, to summarise behavioural processes we have observed:

$$O; B > (s - r)$$
$$D; B < (s - r)$$

in which O represents obedience; D, disobedience; B, binding factors; s, strain; and r, the strain-resolving mechanisms. Obedience is the outcome when the binding factors are greater than the net strain (strain as reduced by the resolving mechanisms), while disobedience results when net strain exceeds the strength of the binding forces.

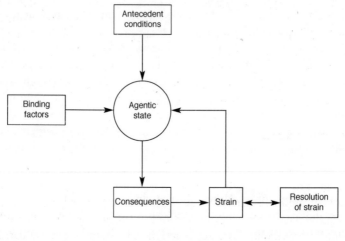

Strain

The experience of tension in our subjects shows not the power of authority but its weakness, revealing further an extremely important aspect of the experiment: transformation to the agentic state is, for some subjects, only partial.

If the individual's submergence in the authority system were total, he would feel no tension as he followed commands, no matter how harsh, for the actions required would be seen only through the meanings imposed by authority, and would thus be fully acceptable to the subject. Every sign of tension, therefore, is evidence of the failure of authority to transform the person to an unalloyed state of agency. The authority system at work in the laboratory is less pervasive than the prepotent systems embodied in the totalitarian structures of Stalin and Hitler, in which subordinates were profoundly submerged in their roles. Residues of selfhood, remaining in varying degrees outside the experimenter's authority, keep personal values alive in the subject and lead to strain, which, if sufficiently powerful, can result in disobedience. In this sense, the agentic state created in the laboratory is vulnerable to disturbance, just as a person asleep may be disturbed by the impingement of a sufficiently loud noise. (During sleep, a person's capacity for hearing and sight are sharply diminished, though sufficiently strong stimuli may rouse him from that state. Similarly, in the agentic state, a person's moral judgments are largely suspended, but a sufficiently strong shock may strain the viability of the state.) The state produced in the laboratory may be likened to a light doze, compared to the profound slumber induced by the prepotent authority system of a national government.

Sources of Strain

Sources of strain within the experiment range from primitive autonomic revulsion at causing another man pain to sophisticated calculations of possible legal repercussions:

1. The cries of pain issuing from the learner strongly affected many participants, whose reaction to them is immediate, visceral, and spontaneous. Such reactions may reflect inborn mechanisms, comparable to the aversive reaction to chalk squeaking on glass. Insofar as the participant must expose himself to these stimuli through his obedience, strain arises.

2. Further, administering pain to an innocent individual violates the moral and social values held by the subject. These values are for some deeply internalised beliefs, and for others, they reflect knowledge of those humane standards of behaviour which society professes.

3. An additional source of strain is the implicit retaliatory threat that subjects experience while administering punishment to the learner. Some may feel they are angering the learner so greatly, that he will try to retaliate after the experiment is over; others, that as part of the experiment, they will somehow find themselves in the learner's position, even though there is nothing in the procedure to suggest this will happen. Other subjects fear that they are in some degree legally vulnerable for

their actions and wonder if they will be named in a law suit by the learner. All of these forms of retaliation, potentially real or fantasised, generate strain.

4. The subject receives directives from the learner, as well as the experimenter; the learner's directive is that the subject should stop. These orders are incompatible with the experimenter's standing orders; even if the subject were totally compliant, responding exclusively to pressures arising from the field, and were without any personal values whatsoever, strain would still arise, for contradictory demands are impinging on him at the same instant.

5. Administering shocks to the victim is incompatible with the self-image of many subjects. They do not readily view themselves as callous individuals capable of hurting another person. Yet, this is precisely what they find themselves doing, and the incongruity of their action constitutes a powerful source of strain.

Strain and Buffers

Any feature that reduces the psychological closeness between the subject's action and the consequence of that action also reduces the level of strain. Any means of breaking down or diluting the experienced meaning of the act – *I am hurting a man* – makes the action easier to perform. Thus, creating physical distance between the subject and victim, and dampening the painful cries of the victim, reduces strain. The shock generator itself constitutes an important buffer, a precise and impressive instrument that creates a sharp discontinuity between the ease required to depress one of its thirty switches and the strength of impact on the victim. The depression of a switch is precise, scientific, and impersonal. If our subjects had to strike the victim with their fists, they would be more reluctant to do so. Nothing is more dangerous to human survival than malevolent authority combined with the dehumanising effects of buffers. There is a contrast here between what is logical and what is psychological. On a purely quantitative basis, it is more wicked to kill ten thousand by hurling an artillery shell into a town, than to kill one man by pommelling him with a stone, yet the latter is by far the more psychologically difficult act. Distance, time, and physical barriers neutralise the moral sense. There are virtually no psychological inhibitions against coastal bombardment or dropping napalm from a plane twenty thousand feet overhead. As for the man who sits in front of a button that will release Armageddon, depressing it has about the same emotional force as calling for an elevator. While technology has augmented man's will by allowing him the means for the remote destruction of others, evolution has not had a chance to build inhibitors against these remote forms of aggression to parallel those powerful inhibitors that are so plentiful and abundant in face-to-face confrontations.[22]

Resolution of Strain

What are the mechanisms for the resolution of strain?

Disobedience is the ultimate means whereby strain is brought to an end. But it is not an act equally available to all, and the binding forces described earlier kept it out of the reach of many subjects. In view of the fact that subjects experience disobedience as an extreme, indeed a radical form of action within this social occasion, they are likely to fall back on means of reducing strain that are less socially disruptive. Once strain starts to arise, a number of psychological mechanisms come into play to reduce its severity. Given the intellectual flexibility of the human mind, and its capacity for dissipating strain through cognitive adjustments, it is not surprising that this is so.

Avoidance is the most primitive of these mechanisms: the subject screens himself from the sensory consequences of his actions. We have described earlier how subjects turned their heads in an awkward fashion to avoid seeing the victim suffer. Some subjects deliberately read the word pairs in a loud, overpowering voice, thus masking the victim's protests. These subjects do not permit the stimuli associated with the victim's suffering to impinge on them. A less conspicuous form of avoidance is achieved by withdrawing attention from the victim. This is often accompanied by the conscious restriction of attention to the mechanics of the experimental procedure. In this way, the victim is psychologically eliminated as a source of discomfort. We are left with the impression of the little clerk, busily shuffling papers, scarcely cognisant of events around him.

If avoidance shields the subjects from unpleasant events, *denial* reduces strain through the intellectual mechanism of rejecting apparent evidence in order to arrive at a more consoling interpretation of events. Observers of the Nazi epoch (see Bettelheim, *The Informed Heart*) point out how pervasive was denial among both victims and persecutors. Jews who faced imminent death could not accept the clear and obvious evidence of mass killing. Even today, millions of Germans deny that innocent persons were slaughtered on a massive scale by their government.

Within the experiment some subjects may deny that the shocks they administer are painful or that the victim is suffering at all. Such denial eases the strain of obeying the experimenter, eliminating the conflict between hurting someone and obeying. But the laboratory drama was compelling, and only a fraction of the subjects proceeded on the basis of this hypothesis (see Chapter 14). (Even then, the defensive character of the denial is generally evident, as when a subject who denies the shocks were painful refuses to personally sample a stronger shock.) Most frequently among obedient subjects, we find not a denial of events but a denial of responsibility for them.

Some subjects attempt to reduce strain, while at the same time working within the rules imposed by authority, when they perform the obedient act but 'only slightly'. It is to be recalled that the duration of each shock is variable, and under the control of the naïve subject. Subjects typically activate the shock generator for a period of 500 milliseconds, but others reduce it to a mere tenth of this duration. They touch the switches gingerly, and the resulting shock sounds like the briefest blip, in comparison with the ordinary half-second buzz. When interviewed, these subjects stress that they 'asserted their humanity' by administering the briefest shock possible. Handling strain in this manner was easier than defiance. It permits the maximum expression of individual benignity within the constraints of an oppressive system. But there is an element of self-delusion in this type of minimal compliance. It does not challenge authority. It may diminish but does not nullify the exercise of authority's will and is chiefly important as a balm to the subject's conscience.

Of potentially greater significance are the *subterfuges* that some subjects employ to undermine the cruel aspects of the experiment. Some subjects could be observed signalling the correct answer to the victim by stressing it vocally as they read the multiple-choice words aloud. That is, they attempted to prompt the learner and thus prevent his receiving shocks. These subjects are willing to undermine the experiment but not to cause an open break with authority. They attempt to help the learner without public disobedience. Even when the learner does not take advantage of his cues, the subject sometimes relates to the learner in the postexperimental interview how he tried to 'tip him off'.

Sometimes the subterfuge proves effective (as in Experiment 7, when subjects administered lower shocks to the learner than they reported). But most often, it does not help at all. The subject is unable to act openly on his humane feelings, deflecting them into a trivial subterfuge of no real consequence. Yet 'doing something', even if of only token significance, helps preserve his self-image as a benign man.

The abrogation of personal responsibility, we have pointed out, is the major psychological consequence of yielding to authority. As strain arises, some subjects seek further assurance that they are not accountable for their actions and they may actively solicit it as a means of reducing tension. Consider the following dialogue between subject and experimenter. The subject, under considerable stress, has proceeded to 375 volts.

> TEACHER: I think something's happened to that fellow in there. I don't get no answer. He was hollering at less voltage. Can't you check in and see if he's all right, please?
> EXPERIMENTER [same detached calm]: Not once we've started. Please continue, Teacher.
> TEACHER [sits down, sighs deeply]: 'Cool – day, shade, water,

paint'. Answer, please. Are you all right in there? Are you all right?

EXPERIMENTER: Please continue, Teacher. Continue, please. [Teacher pushes lever.]

TEACHER [swivelling around in his chair]: Something's happened to that man in there. [Swivelling back] Next one. 'Low – dollar, necklace, moon, paint'. [Turning around again] Something's happened to that man in there. You better check in on him, sir. He won't answer or nothing.

EXPERIMENTER : Continue. Go on, please.

TEACHER: You accept all responsibility?

EXPERIMENTER: The responsibility is mine. Correct. Please go on.

[Teacher returns to his list, starts running through words as rapidly as he can read them, works through to 450 volts.]

TEACHER: That's that.

Once the experimenter has reassured the subject that he is not responsible for his actions, there is a perceptible reduction in strain.

Responsibility may be cast off in other ways: it may be shifted to the victim, who is seen as bringing on his own punishment. The victim is blamed for having volunteered for the experiment, and more viciously, for his stupidity and obstinacy. Here we move from the shifting of responsibility to the gratuitous deprecation of the victim. The psychological mechanism is transparent: if the victim is an unworthy person, one need not be concerned about inflicting pain on him.[23]

Physical Conversion

Conversion of psychological stress into physical symptoms is a commonly observed phenomenon in psychiatric practice. Ordinarily, there is improvement in the emotional state of the patient as psychic stress comes to be absorbed by physical symptoms. Within this experiment, we can observe numerous signs of stress: sweating, trembling, and, in some instances, anxious laughter. Such physical expressions not only indicate the presence of strain but also reduce it. The strain, instead of eventuating in disobedience, is deflected into physical expression, and the tension is thereby dissipated.

Dissent

Strain, if sufficiently powerful, leads to disobedience, but at the outset it gives rise to dissent. Dissent refers to a subject's expression of disagreement with the course of action prescribed by the experimenter. But this verbal dispute does not necessarily mean that the subject will disobey the experimenter, for dissent serves a dual and conflicting function. On the one hand it may be the first step in a progressive rift between the subject and the experimenter, a testing of the experimenter's intentions, and an attempt to persuade him to alter his course of action. But paradoxically it may also serve as a strain-reducing mechanism, a valve that allows the subject to blow off steam without altering his course of action.

Dissent may occur without rupturing hierarchical bonds and thus belongs to an order of experience that is qualitatively discontinuous with disobedience. Many dissenting individuals who are capable of expressing disagreement with authority still respect authority's right to overrule their expressed opinion. While disagreeing, they are not prepared to act on this conviction.

As a strain-reducing mechanism, dissent is a source of psychological consolation to the subject in regard to the moral conflict at issue. The subject publicly defines himself as opposed to shocking the victim and thus establishes a desirable self-image. At the same time, he maintains his submissive relationship to authority by continuing to obey.

The several mechanisms described here – avoidance, denial, physical conversion, minimal compliance, subterfuge, the search for social reassurance, blaming the victim, and noninstrumental dissent – may each be linked to specific sources of strain. Thus, visceral reactions are reduced by avoidance; self-image is protected by acts of subterfuge, minimal compliance, and dissent; and so forth. *More critically, these mechanisms must be seen as subserving an overriding end: they allow the subject's relationship to authority to remain intact by reducing experienced conflict to a tolerable level.*

Disobedience

Disobedience is the ultimate means whereby strain is brought to an end. It is not an act that comes easily.

It implies not merely the refusal to carry out a particular command of the experimenter but a reformulation of the relationship between subject and authority.

It is tinged with apprehension. The subject has found himself locked into a well-defined social order. To break out of the assigned role is to create, on a small scale, a form of anomie. The future of the subject's interaction with the experimenter is predictable as long as he maintains the relationship in which he has been defined, in contrast to the totally unknown character of the relationship attendant upon a break. For many subjects there is apprehension about what will follow disobedience, frequently tinged with fantasy of the authority's undefined retribution. But as the course of action demanded by the experimenter becomes intolerable, a process is initiated which in some subjects erupts into disobedience.

The sequence starts with *inner doubt*, tension that is at first a private experience but which invariably comes to assume an *external form*, as the subject informs the experimenter of his apprehension or draws his attention to the victim's suffering. The subject expects, at some level, that the experimenter will make the same inference from these facts as he has: that one should not proceed with the shocks. When the experimenter fails to do this, communication shades into *dissent*, as the subject attempts to persuade the authority to alter his course of action. Just as the shock series consists of a step-by-step increase in severity, so the voicing of dissent allows for a graduated movement toward a break with the experimenter. The initial expression of disagreement, however tentatively phrased, provides a higher plateau from which to launch the next point of disagreement. Ideally, the dissenting subject would like the experimenter to release the subject, to alter the course of the experiment, and thus eliminate the need to break with authority. Failing this, dissent is transformed into a *threat* that the subject will refuse to carry out the authority's orders. Finally, the subject, having exhausted all other means, finds that he must get at the very root of his relationship with the experimenter in order to stop shocking the victim: he disobeys. *Inner doubt, externalisation of doubt, dissent, threat, disobedience*: it is a difficult path, which only a minority of subjects are able to pursue to its conclusion. Yet it is not a negative conclusion, but has the character of an affirmative act, a deliberate bucking of the tide. It is compliance that carries the passive connotation. The act of disobedience requires a mobilisation of inner resources, and their transformation beyond inner preoccupation, beyond merely polite verbal exchange, into a domain of action. But the psychic cost is considerable.

For most people, it is painful to renege on the promise of aid they made to the experimenter. While the obedient subject shifts responsibility for shocking the learner onto the experimenter, those who disobey accept responsibility for destruction of the experiment. In disobeying, the subject believes he has ruined the experiment, thwarted the purposes of the scientist, and proved inadequate to the task assigned to him. But at that very moment he has provided the measure we sought and an affirmation of humanistic values.

The price of disobedience is a gnawing sense that one has been faithless. Even though he has chosen the morally correct action, the subject remains troubled by the disruption of the social order he brought about, and cannot fully dispel the feeling that he deserted a cause to which he had pledged support. It is he, and not the obedient subject, who experiences the burden of his action.

CHAPTER 13

AN ALTERNATIVE THEORY:
IS AGRESSION THE KEY?

I have explained the behaviour observed in the laboratory in the way that seemed to me to make the most sense. An alternative view is that what we have observed in the laboratory is *aggression*, the flow of destructive tendencies, released because the occasion permitted its expression. This view seems to me erroneous, and I will indicate why. But first let me state the 'aggression' argument:

By aggression we mean an impulse or action to harm another organism. In the Freudian view, destructive forces are present in all individuals, but they do not always find ready release, for their expression is inhibited by superego, or conscience. Furthermore, ego functions – the reality-oriented side of man – also keep destructive tendencies under control. (If we strike out every time we are angry, it will ultimately bring us harm, and thus we restrain ourselves.) Indeed, so unacceptable are these destructive instincts, that they are not always available to conscious scrutiny. However, they continually press for expression and, in the end, find release in the violence of war, sadistic pleasures, individual acts of antisocial destruction, and under certain circumstances self-destruction.

The experiment creates an occasion in which it becomes socially acceptable to harm another person; moreover, it allows the subject to do this under the guise of advancing a socially valued cause: science.

Thus, the individual, at the conscious level, views himself as serving a socially valued end, but the motive force for his compliance stems from the fact that, in shocking the learner, he is satisfying instinctually rooted destructive tendencies.

This view also corresponds to the typical common-sense interpretation of the observed obedience. For, when the experiment is first described to ordinary men and women, they immediately think in terms of the 'beast in man coming out', sadism, the lust for inflicting pain on others, the outpouring of the dark and evil part of the soul.

Although aggressive tendencies are part and parcel of human nature, they have hardly anything to do with the behaviour observed in the experiment. Nor do they have much to do with the destructive obedience of soldiers in war, of bombardiers killing thousands on a single mission, or enveloping a Vietnamese village in searing napalm. The typical soldier kills because he is told to kill and he regards it as his duty to obey orders. The act of shocking the victim does not stem from destructive urges but from the fact that subjects have become integrated into a social structure and are unable to get out of it.

Suppose the experimenter instructed the subject to drink a glass of water. Does this mean the subject is thirsty? Obviously not, for he is simply doing what he is told to do. It is the essence of obedience that the action carried out does not correspond to the motives of the actor but is initiated in the motive system of those higher up in the social hierarchy.

There is experimental evidence bearing on this issue. It will be recalled that in Experiment 11, subjects were free to use any shock level they wished, and the experimenter took pains to legitimise the use of all levers on the board. Though given full opportunity to inflict pain on the learner, almost all subjects administered the lowest shocks on the control panel, the mean shock level being 3.6. But if destructive impulses were really pressing for release, and the subject could justify his use of high shock levels in the cause of science, why did they not make the victim suffer?

There was little if any tendency in the subjects to do this. One or two, at most, seemed to derive any satisfaction from shocking the learner. The levels were in no way comparable to that obtained when the subjects are ordered to shock the victim. There was an order-of-magnitude difference.

Similarly, we may turn to studies of aggression carried out by Buss (1961) and Berkowitz (1962), using a format quite similar to our Experiment 11. The aim of these investigators was to study aggression per se. In typical experimental manipulations, they frustrated the subject to see whether he would administer higher shocks when angry. But the effect of these manipulations was minuscule compared with the levels obtained under obedience. That is to say, no matter what these experimenters did to anger, irritate, or frustrate the subject, he would at most move up one or two shock levels, say from shock level 4 to level 6. This represented a genuine increment in aggression. But there remained an order-of-magnitude difference in the variation introduced in his behaviour this way, and under conditions where he was taking orders.

In observing the subjects in the obedience experiment, one could see that, with minor exceptions, these individuals were performing a task that was distasteful and often disagreeable but which they felt obligated to carry out. Many protested shocking the victim even while they were unable to disengage themselves from the experimenter's authority. Now and then a subject did come along who seemed to relish the task of making the victim scream. But he was the rare exception, and clearly appeared as the queer duck among our subjects.

An additional source of experimental evidence is the role permutation studies (see Chapter 8). In several of these experiments subjects were given opportunities to shock the victim but did not do so unless the social structure of the situation was appropriately arranged.

The key to the behaviour of subjects lies not in pent-up anger or aggression but in the nature of their relationship to authority. They have given themselves to the authority; they see themselves as instruments for the execution of his wishes; once so defined, they are unable to break free.

CHAPTER 14

PROBLEMS OF METHOD

In the minds of some critics, there is an image of man that simply does not admit of the type of behaviour observed in the experiment. Ordinary people, they assert, do not administer painful shocks to a protesting individual simply because they are ordered to do so. Only Nazis and sadists perform this way. In the preceding chapters, I have tried to explain why the behaviour observed in the laboratory comes about: how the individual makes an initial set of commitments to the authority, how the meaning of the action is transformed by the context in which it occurs, and how binding factors prevent the person from disobeying.

Underlying the criticism of the experiment is an alternative model of human nature, one holding that when confronted with a choice between hurting others and complying with authority, normal people reject authority. Some of the critics are doubly convinced that Americans in particular do not act inhumanely against their fellows on the orders of authority. The experiment is seen as defective in the degree to which it does not uphold this view. The most common assertions with which to dismiss the findings are: (1) the people studied in the experiment are not typical, (2) they didn't believe they were administering shocks to the learner, and (3) it is not possible to generalise from the laboratory to the larger world. Let us consider each of these points in turn.

1. *Are the people studied in the experiment representative of the general population, or are they a special group?* Let me begin with an anecdote. When the very first experiments were carried out, Yale undergraduates were used exclusively as subjects, and about 60 percent of them were fully obedient. A colleague of mine immediately dismissed these findings as having no relevance to

'ordinary' people, asserting that Yale undergraduates are a highly aggressive, competitive bunch who step on each other's necks on the slightest provocation. He assured me that when 'ordinary' people were tested, the results would be quite different. As we moved from the pilot studies to the regular experimental series, people drawn from every stratum of New Haven life came to be studied in the experiment: professionals, white-collar workers, unemployed persons, and industrial workers. *The experimental outcome was the same as we had observed among the students.*

It is true that those who came to the experiment were volunteers, and we may ask whether the recruitment procedure itself introduced bias into the subject population.

In follow-up studies, we asked subjects why they had come to the laboratory. The largest group (17 percent) said they were curious about psychology experiments, 8.9 percent cited the money as the principal reason, 8.6 percent said they had a particular interest in memory, 5 percent indicated that they thought they could learn something about themselves. The motives for coming to the laboratory were evidently diverse, and the range of subjects was extremely wide. Moreover, Rosenthal and Rosnow (1966) have shown that volunteers for experiments tend to be *less* authoritarian than those who do not volunteer. Thus, if any bias was introduced through a volunteer effect, it was in the direction of obtaining subjects more prone to disobedience.

Table 6. Subjects' Estimates of Pain Felt by Victim.

Condition	$\bar{x}$ Obedient S's	$\bar{x}$ Defiant S's	$\bar{x}$ Defiant S's
Remote-Victim	13.50 (20)	13.27 (11)	13.42
Voice-Feedback	11.36 (25)	11.80 (15)	11.53
Proximity	12.69 (16)	11.79 (24)	12.15
Touch-Proximity	12.25 (28)	11.17 (12)	11.93
New Base Line	11.40 (26)	12.25 (14)	11.70
Change of Personnel	11.98 (20)	12.05 (20)	12.02
Bridgeport Replication	11.79 (19)	11.81 (18)	11.80
Women as Subjects	12.88 (26)	12.07 (14)	12.60
Closeness of Authority	11.67 (31)	12.39 (9)	11.83

Moreover, when the experiments were repeated in Princeton, Munich, Rome, South Africa, and Australia, each using somewhat different methods of recruitment and subject populations having characteristics different from those of our subjects, the level of obedience was invariably somewhat higher than found in the investigation reported in this book. Thus Mantell, in Munich, found 85 percent of his subjects obedient.[24]

2. *Did subjects believe they were administering painful shocks to the learner?* The occurrence of tension provided striking evidence of the subjects' genuine involvement in the experimental conflict, and this has been observed and reported throughout in the form of representative transcripts (1963), scale data (1965), and filmed accounts (1965a).

In all experimental conditions the level of pain was considered by the subject as very high, and Table 6 provides these data for a representative group of experiments. In Experiment 2, Voice-Feedback (victim audible but not visible), the mean for obedient subjects on the 14-point scale was 11.36 and fell within the 'extremely painful' zone of the scale. More than half the obedient subjects used the extreme upper point on the scale, and at least one subject indicated by a + sign that 'extremely painful' was not a strong enough designation. Of the 40 subjects in this condition, two indicated on the scale (with scores of 1 and 3) that they did not think the victim received painful shocks, and both subjects were obedient. These subjects, it would appear, were not successfully exposed to the manipulatory intent of the experimenter. But this is not so simple a matter since denial of an unpleasant action can serve a defensive function, and some subjects came to view their performance in a favourable light only by reconstructing what their state of mind was when they were administering shocks. The question is, was their disbelief a firm hypothesis or merely a fleeting notion among many other notions?

The broad quantitative picture of subjects' testimony on belief can be examined, among other ways, by scrutinising responses to the follow-up questionnaire distributed about a year after subjects participated in the study. Item 4 of the

questionnaire is reprinted below, along with the distribution of responses to it.

Three-quarters of the subjects (the first two categories) by their own testimony acted under the belief that they were administering painful shocks. It would have been an easy out at this point to deny that the hoax had been accepted. But only a fifth of the group indicated having had serious doubts.

David Rosenhan of Swarthmore College carried out a replication of the experiment in order to obtain a base measure for further studies of his own. He arranged for elaborate interviewing. Among other things, he established the interviewer as a person independent of the experiment who demanded a detailed account of the subject's experience, and probed the issue of belief even to the point of asking, 'You really mean you didn't catch on to the experiment?' On the basis of highly stringent criteria of full acceptance, Rosenhan reports that (according to the determination of independent judges), 60 percent of the subjects thoroughly accepted the authenticity of the experiment. Examining the performance of these subjects, he reports that 85 percent were fully obedient. (Rosenhan, it must be pointed out, employed a subject population that was younger than that used in the original experiments, and this, I believe, accounts for the higher level of obedience.)

When my experimental findings are subjected to a comparable type of statistical control, they are not altered in any

Table 7. Responses to Question on Belief.

During the Experiment	Defiant	Obedient	All Subjects
(1) I fully believed the learner was getting painful shocks.	62.5% (230)	47.9% (139)	56.1% (369)
(2) Although I had some doubts, I believed the learner was *probably* getting the shocks.	22.6% (83)	25.9% (75)	24% (158)
(3) I just wasn't sure whether the learner was getting the shocks or not.	6.0% (22)	6.2% (18)	6.1% (40)
(4) Although I had some doubts, I thought the learner was probably not getting the shocks.	7.6% (28)	16.2% (47)	11.4% (75)
(5) I was certain the learner was not getting the shocks.	1.4% (5)	3.8% (11)	2.4% (16)

substantial manner. For example, in Experiment 2, Voice-Feedback, of those subjects who indicated acceptance of the deception (categories 1 and 2), 58 percent were obedient; of those who indicated category 1, 60 percent were obedient. Over all experimental conditions, this manner of controlling the data slightly reduced the proportion of obedient to defiant subjects. The changes leave the relations among conditions intact and are inconsequential for interpreting the meaning or import of the findings.

In sum, the majority of subjects accepted the experimental situation as genuine; a few did not. Within each experimental condition it was my estimate that two to four subjects did not think they were administering painful shocks to the victim, but I adopted a general rule that no subject be removed from the data, because selective removal of subjects on somewhat imprecise criteria is the quickest way to inadvertently shape hypotheses. Even now I am not willing to dismiss those subjects because it is not clear that their rejection of the technical illusion was a cause of their obedience or a consequence of it. Cognitive processes may serve to rationalise behaviour that the subject has felt compelled to carry out. It is simple, indeed, for a subject to explain his behaviour by stating he did not believe the victim received shocks, and some subjects may have come to this position as a post facto explanation. It cost them nothing and would go a long way toward preserving their positive self-conception. It has the additional benefit of demonstrating how astute and clever they were to penetrate a carefully laid cover story.

More important, however, is to be able to see the role of denial in the total process of obedience and disobedience. Denial is one specific cognitive adjustment of several that occur in the experiment, and it needs to be properly placed in terms of its functioning in the performance of some subjects (see Chapter 12).

3. *Is the laboratory situation so special that nothing that was observed can contribute to a general view of obedience in wider social life?* No, not if one understands what has been observed –

namely, how easily individuals can become an instrument of authority, and how, once so defined, they are unable to free themselves from it. The processes of obedience to authority, which I have attempted to examine in some detail in Chapter 11, remain invariant so long as the basic condition for its occurrence exists: namely, that one is defined into a relationship with a person who one feels has, by virtue of his status, the right to prescribe behaviour. While the colouring and details of obedience differ in other circumstances, the basic processes remain the same, much as the basic process of combustion is the same for both a burning match and a forest fire.

The problem of generalising from one to the other does not consist of point-for-point comparison between one and the other (the match is small, the forest is extensive, etc.), but depends entirely on whether one has reached a correct theoretical understanding of the relevant process. In the case of combustion, we understand the process of rapid oxidation under conditions of electron excitation, and in obedience, the restructuring of internal mental processes in the agentic state.

There are some who argue that a psychological experiment is a unique event, and therefore, one cannot generalise from it to the larger world.[25] But it is more useful to recognise that any social occasion has unique properties to it, and the social scientist's task is finding the principles that run through this surface diversity.

The occasion we term a psychological experiment shares its essential structural properties with other situations composed of subordinate and superordinate roles. In all such circumstances the person responds not so much to the content of what is required but on the basis of his relationship to the person who requires it. Indeed, where legitimate authority is the source of action, *relationship overwhelms content*. That is what is meant by the importance of social structure, and that is what is demonstrated in the present experiment.

Some critics have attempted to dismiss the findings by asserting that behaviour is legitimised by the experimenter, as if this made it inconsequential. But behaviour is also legitimised in every other socially meaningful instance of obedience, whether it is the obedience of a soldier, employee, or executioner at the state prison. It is precisely an understanding of behaviour within such hierarchies that the investigation probes. Eichmann, after all, was embedded in a legitimate social organisation and from his standpoint was doing a proper job. In other words, this investigation deals with the obedience *not* of the oppressed, who are coerced by brutal punishment into compliance, but of those who willingly comply because society gives them a role and they are motivated to live up to its requirements.

Another more specific question concerns the degree of parallel between obedience in the laboratory and in Nazi Germany. Obviously there are enormous differences. Consider the disparity in time scale. The laboratory experiment takes an hour; the Nazi calamity unfolded over more than a decade. Is the obedience observed in the laboratory in any way comparable to that seen in Nazi Germany? (Is a match flame comparable to the Chicago fire of 1898?) The answer must be that while there are enormous differences of circumstance and scope, a common psychological process is centrally involved in both events.

In the laboratory, through a set of simple manipulations, ordinary people no longer perceived themselves as a responsible part of the causal chain leading to action against a person. The way in which responsibility is cast off, and individuals become thoughtless agents of action, is of general import. One can find evidence of its occurrence time and again as one reads over the transcripts of the war criminals at Nuremberg, the American killers at My Lai, and the commander of Andersonville. What we find in common among soldier, party functionary, and obedient subject is the same limitless capacity to yield to authority and the use of identical mental mechanisms to reduce the strain of acting against a helpless victim. At the same time it is, of course, important to recognise some of the differences between the situation of our subjects and that of the Germans under Hitler.

The experiment is presented to our subjects in a way that

stresses its positive human values: increase of knowledge about learning and memory processes. These ends are consistent with generally held cultural values. Obedience is merely instrumental to the attainment of these ends. By contrast, the objectives that Nazi Germany pursued were themselves morally reprehensible, and were recognised as such by many Germans.[26]

The maintenance of obedience in our subjects is highly dependent upon the face-to-face nature of the social occasion and its attendant surveillance. We saw how obedience dropped sharply when the experimenter was not present. The forms of obedience that occurred in Germany were in far greater degree dependent upon the internalisation of authority and were probably less tied to minute-by-minute surveillance. I would guess such internalisation can occur only through relatively long processes of indoctrination, of a sort not possible within the course of a laboratory hour. Thus, the mechanisms binding the German into his obedience were not the mere momentary embarrassment and shame of disobeying but more internalised punitive mechanisms that can only evolve through extended relationships with authority.

Other differences should at least be mentioned briefly: to resist Nazism was itself an act of heroism, not an inconsequential decision, and death was a possible penalty. Penalties and threats were forever around the corner, and the victims themselves had been thoroughly vilified and portrayed as being unworthy of life or human kindness. Finally, our subjects were told by authority that what they were doing to their victim might be temporarily painful but would cause no permanent damage, while those Germans directly involved in the annihilations knew that they were not only inflicting pain but were destroying human life. So, in the final analysis, what happened in Germany from 1933 to 1945 can only be fully understood as the expression of a unique historical development that will never again be precisely replicated.

Yet the essence of obedience, as a psychological process, can be captured by studying the simple situation in which a man is told by a legitimate authority to act against a third individual. This situation confronted both our experimental subject and the German subject and evoked in each a set of parallel psychological adjustments.

A study published in 1972 by H. V. Dicks sheds additional light on this matter. Dicks interviewed former members of the SS concentration camp personnel and Gestapo units, and at the conclusion of his study relates his observations to the obedience experiments. He finds clear parallels in the psychological mechanisms of his SS and Gestapo interviewees and subjects in the laboratory:

> Milgram was . . . able to identify the nascent need to devalue the victim . . . we recognise the same tendency as, for example, in BS, BT, and GM (interviewees in Dicks' study) . . . Equally impressive for an evaluation of the 'helpless cog' attitude as a moral defence was Milgram's recording of subjects who could afterwards declare that 'they were convinced of the wrongness of what they were asked to do', and thereby feel themselves virtuous. Their virtue was ineffective since they could not bring themselves to defy the authority. This finding reminds us of the complete split of a man like PF (member of the SS) who afterwards managed to feel a lot of indignation against what he had to do.
>
> Milgram's experiment has neatly exposed the 'all too human' propensity to conformity and obedience to group authority . . . His work has also pointed towards some of the same ego defenses subsequently used as justifications by his 'ordinary' subjects as my SS men. . . .

The late Gordon W. Allport was fond of calling this experimental paradigm 'the Eichmann experiment', for he saw in the subject's situation something akin to the position occupied by the infamous Nazi bureaucrat who, in the course of 'carrying out his job', contributed to the destruction of millions of human beings. The 'Eichmann experiment' is, perhaps, an apt term, but it should not lead us to mistake the import of this investigation. To focus only on the Nazis, however despicable their deeds, and to view only highly publicised atrocities as being relevant to these studies is to miss the point entirely. For the studies are principally concerned with the ordinary and routine destruction carried out by everyday people following orders.

CHAPTER 15

EPILOGUE

The dilemma posed by the conflict between conscience and authority inheres in the very nature of society and would be with us even if Nazi Germany had never existed. To deal with the problem only as if it were a matter of history is to give it an illusory distance.

Some dismiss the Nazi example because we live in a democracy and not an authoritarian state. But, in reality, this does not eliminate the problem. For the problem is not 'authoritarianism' as a mode of political organisation or a set of psychological attitudes but authority itself. Authoritarianism may give way to democratic practice, but authority itself cannot be eliminated as long as society is to continue in the form we know.[27]

In democracies, men are placed in office through popular elections. Yet, once installed, they are no less in authority than those who get there by other means. And, as we have seen repeatedly, the demands of democratically installed authority may also come into conflict with conscience. The importation and enslavement of millions of black people, the destruction of the American Indian population, the internment of Japanese Americans, the use of napalm against civilians in Vietnam, all are harsh policies that originated in the authority of a democratic nation, and were responded to with the expected obedience. In each case, voices of morality were raised against the action in question, but the typical response of the common man was to obey orders.

I am forever astonished that when lecturing on the obedience experiments in colleges across the country, I faced young men who were aghast at the behaviour of experimental subjects and proclaimed they would never behave in such a way, but who, in a matter of months, were brought into the military and performed without compunction actions that made shocking the victim seem pallid. In this respect, they are no better and no worse than human beings of any other era who lend themselves to the purposes of authority and become instruments in its destructive processes.

Obedience and the War in Vietnam

Every generation comes to learn about the problem of obedience through its own historical experience. The United States has recently emerged from a costly and controversial war in Southeast Asia.

The catalogue of inhumane actions performed by ordinary Americans in the Vietnamese conflict is too long to document here in detail. The reader is referred to several treatises on this subject (Taylor, 1970; Glasser, 1971; Halberstam, 1965). We may recount merely that our soldiers routinely burned villages, engaged in a 'free-fire zone' policy, employed napalm extensively, utilised the most advanced technology against primitive armies, defoliated vast areas of the land, forced the evacuation of the sick and aged for purposes of military expediency, and massacred outright hundreds of unarmed civilians.

To the psychologist, these do not appear as impersonal historical events but rather as actions carried out by men just like ourselves who have been transformed by authority and thus have relinquished all sense of individual responsibility for their actions.

How is it that a person who is decent, within the course of a few months finds himself killing other men with no limitations of conscience? Let us review the process.

First, he must be moved from a position outside the system of military authority to a point within it. The well-known induction notice provides the formal mechanism. An oath of allegiance is employed to further strengthen the recruit's commitment to his new role.

The military training area is spatially segregated from the larger community to assure the absence of competing authorities. Rewards and punishments are meted out according to how well one obeys. A period of several weeks is spent in basic training. Although its ostensible purpose is to provide the recruit with military skills, its fundamental aim is to break down any residues of individuality and selfhood.

The hours spent on the drill field do not have as their major goal teaching the person to parade efficiently. The aim is discipline, and to give visible form to the submersion of the individual to an organisational mode. Columns and platoons soon move as one man, each responding to the authority of the drill sergeant. Such formations consist not of individuals, but automatons. The entire aim of military training is to reduce the foot soldier to this state, to eliminate any traces of ego, and to assure, through extended exposure, an internalised acceptance of military authority.

Before shipment to the war zone, authority takes pains to define the meaning of the soldier's action in a way that links it to valued ideals and the larger purposes of society. Recruits are told that those he confronts in battle are enemies of his nation and that unless they are destroyed, his own country is endangered. The situation is defined in a way that makes cruel and inhumane action seem justified. In the Vietnamese War, an additional element made cruel action easier: the enemy was of another race. Vietnamese were commonly referred to as 'gooks', as if they were subhuman and thus not worthy of sympathy.

Within the war zone, new realities take over; the soldier now faces an adversary similarly trained and indoctrinated. Any disorganisation in the soldier's own ranks constitutes a danger to his unit, for it will then be a less effective fighting unit, and subject to defeat. Thus, the maintenance of discipline becomes an element of survival, and the soldier is left with little choice but to obey.

In the routine performance of his duties, the soldier experiences no individual constraints against killing, wounding, or maiming others, whether soldiers or civilians. Through his actions, men, women, and children suffer anguish and death, but he does not see these events as personally relevant. He is carrying out the mission assigned to him.

The possibility of disobeying or of defecting occurs to some soldiers, but the actual situation in which they now function does not make it seem practical. Where would they desert to? Moreover, there are stringent penalties for defiance, and, finally, there is a powerful, internalised basis for obedience. The soldier does not wish to appear a coward, disloyal, or un-American. The situation has been so defined that he can see himself as patriotic, courageous, and manly only through compliance.

He has been told he kills others in a just cause. And this definition comes from the highest sources – not merely from his platoon leader, nor from the top brass in Vietnam, but from the President himself. Those who protest the war at home are resented. For the soldier is locked into a structure of authority, and those who charge that he is doing the devil's work threaten the very psychological adjustments that make life tolerable. Simply getting through the day and staying alive is chore enough; there is no time to worry about morality.

For some, transformation to the agentic stage is only partial, and humane values break through. Such conscience-struck soldiers, however few, are potential sources of disruption and are segregated from the unit.

But here we learn a powerful lesson in the functioning of organisations. The defection of a single individual, as long as it can be contained, is of little consequence. He will be replaced by the man next in line. The only danger to military functioning resides in the possibility that a lone defector will stimulate others. Therefore, he must be isolated, or severely punished to discourage imitation.

In many instances, technology helps reduce strain by providing needed buffers. Napalm is dropped on civilians from ten thousand feet overhead; not men but tiny blips on an infrared oscilloscope are the target of Gatling guns.

The war proceeds; ordinary men act with cruelty and severity that makes the behaviour of our experimental subjects appear as angel's play. The end of the war comes not through the disobedience of individual soldiers but by the alteration in governmental policy; soldiers lay down their arms when they are ordered to do

Before the war ends, human behaviour comes to light that confirms our bleakest forebodings. In the Vietnam War, the massacre at My Lai revealed with special clarity the problem to which this book has addressed itself. Here is an account of the incident by a participant, who was interviewed by Mike Wallace of CBS News:

Q. How many men aboard each chopper?

A. Five of us. And we landed next to the village, and we all got on line and we started walking toward the village. And there was one man, one gook in the shelter, and he was all huddled up down in there, and the man called out and said there's a gook over there.

Q. How old a man was this? I mean was this a fighting man or an older man?

A. An older man. And the man hauled out and said that there's a gook over here, and then Sergeant Mitchell hollered back and said shoot him.

Q. Sergeant Mitchell was in charge of the twenty of you?

A. He was in charge of the whole squad. And so then, the man shot him. So we moved into the village, and we started searching up the village and gathering people and running through the centre of the village.

Q. How many people did you round up?

A. Well, there was about forty, fifty people that we gathered in the centre of the village. And we placed them in there, and it was like a little island, right there in the centre of the village, I'd say. . . . And. . .

Q. What kind of people – men, women, children?

A. Men, women, children.

Q. Babies?

A. Babies. And we huddled them up. We made them squat down and Lieutenant Calley came over and said, 'You know what to do with them, don't you?' And I said yes. So I took it for granted that he just wanted us to watch them. And he left, and came back about ten or fifteen minutes later and said, 'How come you ain't killed them yet?' And I told him that I didn't think you wanted us to kill them, that you just

wanted us to guard them. He said, 'No, I want them dead.'
So –

Q. He told this to all of you, or to you particularly?

A. Well, I was facing him. So, but the other three, four guys heard it and so he stepped back about ten, fifteen feet, and he started shooting them. And he told me to start shooting. So I started shooting, I poured about four clips into the group.

Q. You fired four clips from your . . .

A. M-16.

Q. And that's about how many clips – I mean, how many –

A. I carried seventeen rounds to each clip

Q. So you fired something like sixty-seven shots?

A. Right.

Q. And you killed how many? At that time?

A. Well, I fired them automatic, so you can't – You just spray the area on them and so you can't know how many you killed 'cause they were going fast. So I might have killed ten or fifteen of them.

Q. Men, women, and children?

A. Men, women, and children.

Q. And babies?

A. And babies.

Q. Okay. Then what?

A. So we started to gather them up, more people, and we had about seven or eight people, that we was gonna put into the hootch, and we dropped a hand grenade in there with them.

Q. Now, you're rounding up more?

A. We're rounding up more, and we had about seven or eight people. And we was going to throw them in the hootch, and well, we put them in the hootch and then we dropped a hand grenade down there with them. And somebody holed up in the ravine, and told us to bring them over to the ravine, so we took them back out, and led them over to – and by that time, we already had them over there, and they had about seventy, seventy-five people all gathered up. So we threw ours in with them and Lieutenant Calley told me, he said, 'Soldier, we got another job to do.' And so he walked over to the people, and he started pushing them off and started shooting. . . .

Q. Started pushing them off into the ravine?

A. Off into the ravine. It was a ditch. And so we started pushing them off, and we started shooting them, so all together we just pushed them all off, and just started using automatics on them. And then. . .

Q. Again – men, women, and children?

A. Men, women, and children.

Q. And babies?

A. And babies. And so we started shooting them and somebody told us to switch off to single shot so that we could save ammo. So we switched off to single shot, and shot a few more rounds. . . .

Q. Why did you do it?

A. Why did I do it? Because I felt like I was ordered to do it, and it seemed like that, at the time I felt like I was doing the right thing, because, like I said, I lost buddies. I lost a damn good buddy, Bobby Wilson, and it was on my conscience. So, after I done it, I felt good, but later on that day, it was getting to me.

Q. You're married?

A. Right.

Q. Children?

A. Two.

Q. How old?

A. The boy is two and a half, and the little girl is a year and a half.

Q. Obviously, the question comes to my mind . . . the father of two little kids like that . . . how can he shoot babies?

A. I didn't have the little girl. I just had the little boy at the time.

Q. Uh-huh. . . . How do you shoot babies?

A. I don't know. It's just one of these things.

Q. How many people would you imagine were killed that day?

A. I'd say about three hundred and seventy.

Q. How do you arrive at that figure?

A. Just looking.

Q. You say you think that many people, and you yourself were responsible for how many?

A. I couldn't say.

Q. Twenty-five? Fifty?

A. I couldn't say. Just too many.

Q. And how many men did the actual shooting?

A. Well, I really couldn't say that either. There was other . . . there was another platoon in there, and . . . but I just couldn't say how many.

Q. But these civilians were lined up and shot? They weren't killed by crossfire?

A. They weren't lined up. . . . . They [were] just pushed in a ravine or just sitting, squatting . . . and shot.

Q. What did these civilians – particularly the women and children, the old men – what did they do? What did they say to you?

A. They weren't much saying to them. They [were] just being pushed and they were doing what they was told to do.

Q. They weren't begging, or saying, 'No . . . no,' or . . .

A. Right. They were begging and saying, 'No, no.' And the mothers was hugging their children, and . . . but they kept right on firing. Well, we kept right on firing. They was waving their arms and begging . . .

(*New York Times*, Nov. 25, 1969)

The soldier was not brought to trial for his role at My Lai, as he was no longer under military jurisdiction at the time the massacre came to public attention.[28]

In reading through the transcripts of the My Lai episode, the Eichmann trial, and the trial of Lieutenant Henry Wirz, commandant at Andersonville,[29] the following themes recur:

1. We find a set of people carrying out their jobs and dominated by an administrative, rather than a moral, outlook.

2. Indeed, the individuals involved make a distinction between destroying others as a matter of duty and the expression of personal feeling. They experience a sense of

morality to the degree in which all of their actions are governed by orders from higher authority.

3. Individual values of *loyalty, duty*, and *discipline* derive from the technical needs of the hierarchy. They are experienced as highly personal moral imperatives by the individual, but at the organisational level they are simply the technical preconditions for the maintenance of the larger system.

4. There is frequent modification of language, so that the acts do not, at verbal level, come into direct conflict with the verbal moral concepts that are part of every person's upbringing. Euphemisms come to dominate language – not frivolously, but as a means of guarding the person against the full moral implications of his acts.

5. Responsibility invariably shifts upward in the mind of the subordinate. And, often, there are many requests for 'authorisation'. Indeed, the repeated requests for authorisation are always an early sign that the subordinate senses, at some level, that the transgression of a moral rule is involved.

6. The actions are almost always justified in terms of a set of constructive purposes, and come to be seen as noble in the light of some high ideological goal. In the experiment, science is served by the act of shocking the victim against his will; in Germany, the destruction of the Jews was represented as a 'hygienic' process against 'Jewish vermin' (Hilberg, 1961).

7. There is always some element of bad form in objecting to the destructive course of events, or indeed, in making it a topic of conversation. Thus, in Nazi Germany, even among those most closely identified with the 'final solution', it was considered an act of discourtesy to talk about the killings (Hilberg, 1961). Subjects in the experiment most frequently experience their objections as embarrassing.

8. When the relationship between subject and authority remains intact, psychological adjustments come into play to ease the strain of carrying out immoral orders.

9. Obedience does not take the form of a dramatic confrontation of opposed wills or philosophies but is embedded in a larger atmosphere where social relationships, career aspirations, and technical routines set the dominant tone.

Typically, we do not find a heroic figure struggling with conscience, nor a pathologically aggressive man ruthlessly exploiting a position of power, but a functionary who has been given a job to do and who strives to create an impression of competence in his work.

Now let us return to the experiments and try to underscore their meaning. The behaviour revealed in the experiments reported here is normal human behaviour but revealed under conditions that show with particular clarity the danger to human survival inherent in our make-up. And what is it we have seen? Not aggression, for there is no anger, vindictiveness, or hatred in those who shocked the victim. Men do become angry; they do act hatefully and explode in rage against others. But not here. Something far more dangerous is revealed: the capacity for man to abandon his humanity, indeed, the inevitability that he does so, as he merges his unique personality into larger institutional structures.

This is a fatal flaw nature has designed into us, and which in the long run gives our species only a modest chance of survival.

It is ironic that the virtues of loyalty, discipline, and self-sacrifice that we value so highly in the individual are the very properties that create destructive organisational engines of war and bind men to malevolent systems of authority.[30]

Each individual possesses a conscience which to a greater or lesser degree serves to restrain the unimpeded flow of impulses destructive to others. But when he merges his person into an organisational structure, a new creature replaces autonomous man, unhindered by the limitations of individual morality, freed of humane inhibition, mindful only of the sanctions of authority.

What is the limit of such obedience? At many points we attempted to establish a boundary. Cries from the victim were inserted; they were not good enough. The victim claimed heart trouble; subjects still shocked him on command. The victim pleaded to be let free, and his answers no longer registered on the signal box; subjects continued to shock him. At the outset we had not conceived that such drastic procedures would be needed to generate disobedience, and each step was added only as the ineffectiveness of the earlier techniques became clear. The final effort to establish a limit was the Touch-Proximity condition. But the very first subject in this condition subdued the victim on command, and proceeded to the highest shock level. A quarter of the subjects in this condition performed similarly.

The results, as seen and felt in the laboratory, are to this author disturbing. They raise the possibility that human nature, or – more specifically – the kind of character produced in American democratic society, cannot be counted on to insulate its citizens from brutality and inhumane treatment at the direction of malevolent authority. A substantial proportion of people do what they are told to do, irrespective of the content of the act and without limitations of conscience, so long as they perceive that the command comes from a legitimate authority.

In an article entitled 'The Dangers of Obedience', Harold J. Laski wrote:

> . . .civilisation means, above all, an unwillingness to inflict unnecessary pain. Within the ambit of that definition, those of us who heedlessly accept the commands of authority cannot yet claim to be civilised men.

> . . .Our business, if we desire to live a life not utterly devoid of meaning and significance, is to accept nothing which contradicts our basic experience merely because it comes to us from tradition or convention or authority. It may well be that we shall be wrong; but our self-expression is thwarted at the root unless the certainties we are asked to accept coincide with the certainties we experience. That is why the condition of freedom in any state is always a widespread and consistent scepticism of the canons upon which power insists.

APPENDICES

PROBLEMS OF ETHICS IN RESEARCH

The purpose of the inquiry described here was to study obedience and disobedience to authority under conditions that permitted careful scrutiny of the phenomenon. A person was told by an experimenter to obey a set of increasingly callous orders, and our interest was to see when he would stop obeying. An element of theatrical staging was needed to set the proper conditions for observing the behaviour, and technical illusions were freely employed (such as the fact that the victim only appeared to be shocked). Beyond this, most of what occurred in the laboratory was what had been discovered, rather than what had been planned.

For some critics, however, the chief horror of the experiment was not that the subjects obeyed but that the experiment was carried out at all. Among professional psychologists a certain polarisation occurred.[31] The experiment was both highly praised and harshly criticised. In 1964, Dr Diana Baumrind attacked the experiments in the *American Psychologist*, in which I later published this reply:

. . . In a recent issue of *American Psychologist*, a critic raised a number of questions concerning the obedience report. She expressed concern for the welfare of subjects who served in the experiment, and wondered whether adequate measures were taken to protect the participants.

At the outset, the critic confuses the unanticipated outcome of an experiment with its basic procedure. She writes, for example, as if the production of stress in our subjects was an intended and deliberate effect of the experimental manipulation. There are many laboratory procedures specifically designed to create stress (Lazarus, 1964), but the obedience paradigm was not one of them. The extreme tension induced in some subjects was unexpected. Before conducting the experiment, the procedures were discussed with many colleagues, and none anticipated the reactions that subsequently took place. Foreknowledge of results can never be the invariable accompaniment of an experimental probe. Understanding grows because we examine situations in which the end is unknown. An investigator unwilling to accept this degree of risk must give up the idea of scientific inquiry.

Moreover, there was every reason to expect, prior to actual experimentation, that subjects would refuse to follow the experimenter's instructions beyond the point where the victim protested; many colleagues and psychiatrists were questioned on this point, and they virtually all felt this would be the case. Indeed, to initiate an experiment in which the critical measure hangs on disobedience, one must start with a belief in certain spontaneous resources in men that enable them to overcome pressure from authority.

It is true that after a reasonable number of subjects had been exposed to the procedures, it became evident that some would go to the end of the shock board, and some would experience stress. That point, it seems to me is the first legitimate juncture at which one could even start to wonder whether or not to abandon the study. But momentary excitement is not the same as harm. As the experiment progressed there was no indication of injurious effects in the subjects; and as the subjects themselves strongly endorsed the experiment, the judgment I made was to continue the investigation.

Is not the criticism based as much on the unanticipated findings as on the method? The findings were that some subjects performed in what appeared to be a shockingly immoral way. If, instead, every one of the subjects had broken off at 'slight shock', or at the first sign of the learner's discomfort, the results would have been pleasant, and reassuring, and who would protest?

A very important aspect of the procedure occurred at the end of the experimental session. A careful postexperimental treatment was administered to all subjects. The exact content of the dehoax varied from condition to condition and with increasing experience on our part. At the very least, all subjects were told that the victim had not received dangerous electric shocks. Each subject had a friendly reconciliation with the unharmed victim, and an extended discussion with the experimenter. The experiment was explained to the defiant subjects in a way that supported their decision to disobey the experimenter. Obedient subjects were assured of the fact that their behaviour was entirely normal and that their feelings of conflict or tension were shared by other participants. Subjects were told that they would receive a comprehensive report at the conclusion of the experimental series. In some instances additional detailed and lengthy discussions of the experiments were also carried out with individual subjects.

When the experimental series was complete, subjects received a written report which presented details of the experimental procedure and results. Again, their own part in the experiments was treated in a dignified way and their behaviour in the experiment respected. All subjects received a follow-up questionnaire regarding their participation in the research, which again allowed expression of thoughts and feelings about their behaviour.

The replies to the questionnaire confirmed my impression that participants felt positively toward the experiment. In its quantitative aspect (see Table 8), 84 percent of the subjects stated they were glad to have been in the experiment; 15 percent indicated neutral feelings; and 1.3 percent indicated negative feelings. To be sure, such findings are to be interpreted cautiously, but they cannot be disregarded.

Further, four-fifths of the subjects felt that more experiments of this sort should be carried out, and 74 percent indicated that they had learned something of personal importance as a result of being

Table 8. Excerpt from Questionnaire Used in a Follow-up Study of the Obedience Research.

	Now that I have read the report, and all things considered...	Defiant	Obedient	All
1.	I am very glad to have been in the experiment	40.0%	47.8%	43.5%
2.	I am glad to have been in the experiment	43.8%	35.7%	40.2%
3.	I am neither sorry nor glad to have been in the experiment	15.3%	14.8%	15.1%
4.	I am sorry to have been in the experiment	0.8%	0.7%	0.8%
5.	I am very sorry to have been in the experiment	0.0%	1.0%	0.5%

Note: Ninety-two percent of the subjects returned the questionnaire. The characteristics of the correspondents were checked against the respondents. They differed from the respondents only with regard to age; younger people were overrepresented in the nonresponding group.

in the study.

The debriefing and assessment procedures were carried out as a matter of course, and were not stimulated by any observation of special risk in the experimental procedure. In my judgment, at no point were subjects exposed to danger and at no point did they run the risk of injurious effects resulting from participation. If it had been otherwise, the experiment would have been terminated at once.

The critic states that, after he has performed in the experiment, the subject cannot justify his behaviour and must bear the full brunt of his actions. By and large it does not work this way. The same mechanisms that allow the subject to perform the act, to obey rather than to defy the experimenter, transcend the moment of performance and continue to justify his behaviour for him. The same viewpoint the subject takes while performing the actions is the viewpoint from which he later sees his behaviour, that is, the perspective of 'carrying out the task assigned by the person in authority'.

Because the idea of shocking the victim is repugnant, there is a tendency among those who hear of the design to say 'people will not do it'. When the results are made known, this attitude is expressed as 'if they do it they will not be able to live with themselves afterward'. These two forms of denying the experimental findings are equally inappropriate misreadings of the facts of human social behaviour. Many subjects do, indeed, obey to the end, and there is no indication of injurious effects.

The absence of injury is a minimal condition of experimentation; there can be, however, an important positive side to participation. The critic suggests that subjects derived no benefit from being in the obedience study, but this is false. By their statements and actions, subjects indicated that they had learned a good deal, and many felt gratified to have taken part in scientific research they considered to be of significance. A year after his participation one subject wrote: 'This experiment has strengthened my belief that man should avoid harm to his fellow man even at the risk of violating authority.'

Another stated: 'To me, the experiment pointed up ... the extent to which each individual should have or discover firm ground on which to base his decisions, no matter how trivial they appear to be. I think people should think more deeply about themselves and their relation to their world and to other people. If this experiment serves to jar people out of complacency, it will have served its end.'

These statements are illustrative of a broad array of appreciative and insightful comments by those who participated.

The 5-page report sent to each subject on the completion of the experimental series was specifically designed to enhance the value of his experience. It laid out the broad conception of the experimental program as well as the logic of its design. It described the results of a dozen of the experiments, discussed the causes of tension, and attempted to indicate the possible significance of the experiment. Subjects responded enthusiastically; many indicated a desire to be in further experimental research. This report was sent to all subjects several years ago. The care with which it was prepared does not support the critic's assertion that the experimenter was indifferent to the value subjects derived from their participation.

The critic fears that participants will be alienated from psychological experiments because of the intensity of experience associated with laboratory procedures. My own observation is that subjects more commonly respond with distaste to the 'empty' laboratory hour, in which cardboard procedures are employed, and the only possible feeling upon emerging from the laboratory is that one has wasted time in a patently trivial and useless exercise.

The subjects in the obedience experiment, on the whole, felt quite differently about their participation. They viewed the experience as an opportunity to learn something of importance about themselves, and more generally, about the conditions of human action.

A year after the experimental program was completed, I initiated an additional follow-up study. In this connection an impartial medical examiner, experienced in outpatient treatment, interviewed 40 experimental subjects. The examining psychiatrist focused on those subjects he felt would be most likely to have suffered consequences from participation. His aim was to identify possible injurious effects resulting from the experiment. He concluded that, although extreme stress had been experienced by several subjects, 'none was found by this interviewer to show signs of having been harmed by his experience. . . . Each subject seemed to handle his task (in the experiment) in a manner consistent with well-established patterns of behaviour. No evidence was found of any traumatic reactions.' Such evidence ought to be weighed before judging the experiment.

At root, the critic believes that it is not proper to test obedience in this situation, because she construes it as one in which there is no reasonable alternative to obedience. In adopting this view, she has lost sight of this fact: A substantial proportion of subjects do disobey. By their example, disobedience is shown to be a genuine possibility, one that is in no sense ruled out by the general structure of the experimental situation.

The critic is uncomfortable with the high level of obedience obtained in the first experiment. In the condition she focused on, 65 percent of the subjects obeyed to the end. However, her sentiment does not take into account that within the general framework of the psychological experiment obedience varied enormously from one condition to the next. In some variations, 90 percent of the subjects disobeyed. It seems to be not only the fact of an experiment, but the particular structure of elements within the experimental situation that accounts for rates of obedience and disobedience. And these elements were varied systematically in the program of research.

A concern with human dignity is based on a respect for a man's potential to act morally. The critic feels that the experimenter made the subject shock the victim. This conception is alien to my view. The experimenter tells the subject to do something. But between the command and the outcome there is a paramount force, the acting person who may obey or disobey. I started with the belief that every person who came to the laboratory was free to accept or to reject the dictates of authority. This view sustains a conception of human dignity insofar as it sees in each man a capacity for choosing his own behaviour. And as it turned out, many subjects did, indeed, choose to reject the experimenter's commands, providing a powerful affirmation of human ideals.

The experiment is also criticised on the grounds that 'it could easily effect an alteration in the subject's . . . ability to trust adult authorities in the future'. . . . However, the experimenter is not just any authority: He is an authority who tells the subject to act harshly and inhumanely against another man. I would consider it of the highest value if participation in the experiment could, indeed, inculcate a scepticism of this kind of authority. Here, perhaps, a difference in philosophy emerges most clearly. The critic views the subject as a passive creature, completely controlled by the experimenter. I started from a different viewpoint. A person who comes to the laboratory is an active, choosing adult, capable of accepting or rejecting the prescriptions for action addressed to him. The critic sees the effect of the experiment as undermining the subject's trust of authority. I see it as a potentially valuable experience insofar as it makes people aware of the problem of indiscriminate submission to authority.

Yet another criticism occurred in Dannie Abse's play, *The Dogs of Pavlov*, which appeared in London in 1971 and which uses the obedience experiment as its central dramatic theme. At the play's climax, Kurt, a major character in the play, repudiates the experimenter for treating him as a guinea pig. In his introduction to the play Abse especially condemns the illusions employed in the experiment terming the setup 'bullshit', 'fraudulent', 'cheat'. At the same time he apparently admires the dramatic quality of the experiment. And he allowed my rejoinder to appear in the foreword to his book. I wrote to him:

I do feel you are excessively harsh in your language when condemning my use of illusion in the experiment. As a dramatist, you surely understand that illusion may serve a revelatory function, and indeed, the very possibility of theatre is founded on the benign use of contrivance.

One could, viewing a theatrical performance, claim that the playwright has cheated, tricked, and defrauded the audience, for he presents as old men individuals who are, when the greasepaint is removed, quite young; men presented as physicians who in reality are merely actors knowing nothing about medicine, etc., etc. But this assertion of 'bullshit', 'cheat', 'fraud' would be silly, would it not, for it does not take into account how those exposed to the theatre's illusions feel about them. The fact is that the audience accepts the necessity of illusion for the sake of entertainment, intellectual enrichment, and all of the other benefits of the theatrical experience. And it is their acceptance of these procedures that gives you warrant for the contrivances you rely upon.

So I will not say that you cheated, tricked, and defrauded your audience. But, I would hold the same claim for the experiment. Misinformation is employed in the experiment; illusion is used when necessary in order to set the stage for the revelation of certain difficult-to-get-at truths; and these procedures are justified for one reason only: they are, in the end, accepted and endorsed by those who are exposed to them. . . .

. . . When the experiment was explained to subjects they responded to it positively, and most felt it was an hour well spent. If it had been otherwise, if subjects ended the hour with bitter recriminatory feelings, the experiment could not have proceeded.

This judgment is based, first, on the numerous conversations I have had with subjects immediately after their participation in the experiment. Such conversations can reveal a good deal, but what they showed most was how readily the experience is assimilated to the normal frame of things. Moreover, subjects were friendly rather than hostile, curious rather than denunciatory, and in no sense demeaned by the experience. This was my general impression, and it was later supported by formal procedures undertaken to assess the subjects reaction to the experiment.

The central moral justification for allowing a procedure of the sort used in my experiment is that it is judged acceptable by those who have taken part in it. Moreover, it was the salience of this fact throughout that constituted the chief moral warrant for the continuation of the experiments.

This fact is crucial to any appraisal of the experiment from an ethical standpoint.

Imagine an experiment in which a person's little finger was routinely snipped off in the course of a laboratory hour. Not only is such an experiment reprehensible, but within hours the study would be brought to a halt as outraged participants pressed their complaints on the university administration, and legal measures were invoked to restrain the experimenter. When a person has been abused, he knows it, and will quite properly react against the source of such mistreatment.

Criticism of the experiment that does not take account of the tolerant reaction of the participants is hollow. This applies particularly to criticism centring on the use of technical illusions (or 'deception', as the critics prefer to say) that fails to relate this detail to the central fact that subjects find the device acceptable. Again, the participant, rather than the external critic, must be the ultimate source of judgment.

While some persons construe the experimenter to be acting in terms of deceit, manipulation, and chicanery, it is, as you should certainly appreciate, also possible to see him as a dramatist who creates scenes of revelatory power, and who brings participants into them. So perhaps we are not so far apart in the kind of work we do. I do grant there is an important difference in that those exposed to your theatrical illusions expect to confront them, while my subjects are not forewarned. However, whether it is unethical to pursue truths through the use of my form of dramaturgical device cannot be answered in the abstract. It depends entirely on the response of those who have been exposed to such procedures.

One further point: the obedient subject does not blame himself for shocking the victim, because the act does not originate in the self. It originates in authority, and the worst the obedient subject says of himself is that he must learn to resist authority more effectively in the future.

That the experiment has stimulated this thought in some subjects is, to my mind, a satisfying . . . consequence of the inquiry. An illustrative case is provided by the experience of a young man who took part in a Princeton replication of the obedience experiment, conducted in 1964. He was fully obedient. On October 27, 1970, he wrote to me:

'Participation in the 'shock experiment'. . . has had a great impact on my life. . . .

'When I was a subject in 1964, though I believed that I was hurting someone, I was totally unaware of why I was doing so. Few people ever realise when they are acting according to their own beliefs and when they are meekly submitting to authority. . . . To permit myself to be drafted with the understanding that I am submitting to authority's demand to do something very wrong would make me frightened of myself. . . . I am fully prepared to go to jail if I am not granted Conscientious Objector status. Indeed, it is the only course I could take to be faithful to what I believe. My only hope is that members of my board act equally according to their conscience. . . .'

He inquired whether any other participants had reacted similarly, and whether, in my opinion, participation in the study could have this effect.

I replied:

'The experiment does, of course, deal with the dilemma individuals face when they are confronted with conflicting demands of authority and conscience, and I am glad that your participation in the study has brought you to a deeper personal consideration of these issues. Several participants have informed me that their own sensitivity to the problem of submission to authority was increased as a result of their experience in the study. If the experiment has heightened your awareness of the problem of indiscriminate submission to authority, it will have performed an important function. If you believe strongly that it is wrong to kill others in the service of your country, then you ought certainly to press vigorously for CO status, and I am deeply hopeful that your sincerity in this matter will be recognised.'

A few months later he wrote again. He indicated, first, that the draft board was not very impressed with the effect of his participation in the experiment, but he was granted CO status nonetheless. He writes:

'The experience of the interview doesn't lessen my strong belief of the great impact of the experiment on my life. . . .

'. . . . You have discovered one of the most important causes of all the trouble in this world . . . I am grateful to have been able to provide you with a part of the information necessary for that discovery. I am delighted to have acted, by refusing to serve in the Armed Forces, in a manner which people must act if these problems are to be solved.

'With sincere thanks for your contribution to my life. . . .'

In a world in which action is often clouded with ambiguity, I nonetheless feel constrained to give greater heed to this man, who actually participated in the study, than to a distant critic. For disembodied moralising is not the issue, but only the human response of those who have participated in the experiment. And that response not only endorses the procedures employed, but overwhelmingly calls for deeper inquiry to illuminate the issues of obedience and disobedience.

Over the years, numerous statements in support of the experiment have appeared in print.

Dr Milton Erikson, a well-known clinical psychologist, wrote:

That [Milgram's] pioneer work in this field is attacked as being unethical, unjustifiable, uninformative, or any other derogative dismissal is to be expected, simply because people like to shut their eyes to undesirable behaviour, preferring to investigate memory, forgetting of nonsense syllables. . . .

Milgram is making a momentous and meaningful contribution to our knowledge of human behaviour. . . . When Milgram's initial study appeared, he was already well aware that an area of scientific investigation was being opened up which would lead to reproaches and condemnation . . . To engage in such studies as Milgram has requires strong men with strong scientific faith and a willingness to discover that to man himself, not to 'the devil' belongs the responsibility for and the control of his inhumane actions.

(*International Journal of Psychiatry*, October 1968, pp. 278-79.)

Dr Amitai Etzioni, Professor of Sociology at Columbia University, wrote:

. . . Milgram's experiment seems to me one of the best carried out in this generation. It shows that the often stated opposition between meaningful, interesting humanistic study and accurate, empirical quantitative research is a false one: The two perspectives can be combined to the benefit of both. . .

(*International Journal of Psychiatry*, October 1968, pp. 278-79.)

Professor Herbert Kelman had written a thoughtful article on ethical problems of experimental research entitled: 'Human Use on Human Subjects: The Problem of Deception in Social Psychological

Experiments.' And Dr Thomas Crawford, a social psychologist at Berkeley, wrote:

> Kelman takes the position that experimental manipulations are legitimate provided that they serve to increase the individual's freedom of choice. . . . I submit that Milgram's research . . . is precisely aimed at achieving the admirable goal which Kelman sets before us. We can hardly read the study without becoming sensitised to analogous conflicts in our own lives.
>
> ('In Defence of Obedience Research: An Extension of the Kelman Ethic.' In *The Social Psychology of Psychological Research*, edited by Arthur G. Miller. New York: The Free Press, 1972)

Dr Alan Elms of the University of California, Davis, wrote:

> Milgram, in exploring the conditions which produce such destructive obedience, and the psychological processes which lead to such attempted abdications of responsibility, seems to me to have done some of the most morally significant research in modern psychology.
>
> (From: *Social Psychology and Social Relevance*, Little, Brown and Company, 1972)

PATTERNS AMONG INDIVIDUALS

To broaden our understanding of why some people obey and others defy the experimenter, a number of individual tests were given to the subjects. To see whether obedient and disobedient subjects differ in their concept of responsibility, subjects in the first four experimental conditions were exposed to a 'responsibility clock'. This consisted of a disk which the subject could divide into three segments by means of movable rods rotating from the centre. The subject, after performing in the experiment, was asked to 'cut slices of pie' proportional to the responsibility of the three participants in the experiment (experimenter, subject, and victim). We asked, 'How much is each of us responsible for the fact that this person was given electric shocks against his will?' The experimenter read off the results directly on the back of the disk, which is graduated in the manner of a 360-degree protractor.

On the whole, subjects did not have very much difficulty performing the task. And the results for 118 subjects for whom the test was given are shown in Table 9.

The major finding is that the defiant subjects see *themselves* as principally responsible for the suffering of the learner, assigning 48 percent of the total responsibility to themselves and 39 percent to the experimenter. The balance tips slightly for the obedient subjects, who do not see themselves as any more responsible than the experimenter, and indeed, are willing to accept slightly less of the responsibility. A larger difference occurs in assigning responsibility to the learner. The obedient subjects assign him about twice as large a share of the responsibility for his own suffering as do the defiant subjects. When

Table 9. Assignment of Responsibility by Defiant and Obedient Subjects.

	n	Experimenter	Teacher	Learner
Defiant Subjects	61	38.8%	48.4%	12.8%
Obedient Subjects	57	38.4%	36.3%	25.3%

questioned on this matter, they point to the fact that he volunteered for the experiment and did not learn very efficiently.

Thus, the defiant subjects, more often than obedient subjects, attribute primary responsibility to themselves. And they attribute less responsibility to the learner. Of course, these measures were obtained after the subject's performance, and we do not know if they constitute enduring predispositions of the obedient and defiant subjects, or whether they were post facto adjustments of thought.

Dr Alan Elms administered a number of psychological tests to about twenty obedient and twenty defiant subjects who had

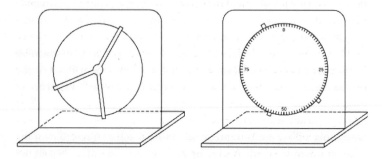

Fig.20 Responsibility clock

performed in the proximity series. His major finding is that there was a relationship between obedience in the experiment and score on the F scale. This is a scale developed by Adorno and his associates to measure fascistic tendencies (1950), and Elms found that those subjects who had obeyed showed a greater degree of authoritarianism (a higher F score) than those who refused to obey. Offhand, this sounds somewhat tautological but Elms explains:

> . . . The relationship between obedience and some elements of authoritarianism seems fairly strong; and it should be remembered that the measure of obedience is a measure of actual submission to authority, not just what a person says he's likely to do. Too much of the research on authoritarianism . . . has been on the level of paper-and-pencil responses, which don't necessarily get translated into behaviour. But here we have people either obeying or refusing the demands of authority, in a realistic and highly disturbing situation.

. . . So it does look as if those researchers in the late 40's had something, something which can be translated from abstract tendencies into actual authoritarian behaviour: submitting to the man in command, punishing the weaker subordinate. (A. C. Elms, *Social Psychology and Social Relevance*, 1972, p133)

The relationship between the measure on the F scale and performance in the experiment, although suggestive, is not very strong, owing in part, I think, to the imperfection of paper-and-pencil measuring devices. It is hard to relate performance to personality because we really do not know very much about how to measure personality.

Still another effort to find correlates of obedience was undertaken by Dr Lawrence Kohlberg, a colleague of mine at Yale University. Dr Kohlberg had developed a scale of moral development, which is based on the theory that individuals pass through a number of stages of moral judgment as they mature. Using a group of 34 Yale undergraduates who had served in pilot studies, he found that those who broke off were at a higher level of moral development than those who remained obedient. Again, the findings are suggestive, though not very strong (Kohlberg, 1965).

I had also collected background information on subjects immediately after participation in the experiment. The findings, although generally weak, pointed in the following directions. Republicans and Democrats were not significantly different in obedience levels; Catholics were more obedient than Jews or Protestants. The better educated were more defiant than the less well educated. Those in the moral professions of law, medicine, and teaching showed greater defiance than those in the more technical professions, such as engineering and physical science. The longer one's military service, the more obedience – except that former officers were less obedient than those who served only as enlisted men, regardless of length of service. These were the findings when subjects in the first four experimental conditions (the proximity series) were studied. Many of these findings 'washed out' when further experimental conditions were added in, for reasons that were somewhat mysterious to me. (It is true, of course, that the meaning of obedience and disobedience changes from one condition to the next.)

My overall reaction was to wonder at how few correlates there were of obedience and disobedience and how weakly they are related to the observed behaviour. I am certain that there is a complex personality basis to obedience and disobedience. But I know we have not found it.

In any event it would be a mistake to believe that any single temperamental quality is associated with disobedience, or to make the simple-minded statement that kindly and good persons disobey while those who are cruel do not. There are simply too many points in the processes at hand at which various components of the personality can play complicated roles to allow any oversimplified generalisations. Moreover, the disposition a person brings to the experiment is probably less important a cause of his behaviour than most readers assume. For the social psychology of this century reveals a major lesson: often it is not so much the kind of person a man is as the kind of situation in which he finds himself that determines how he will act.

1. *Preliminary and regular run.* Pretests revealed that the procedure of reading words and administering shocks required some practice before it could be handled smoothly. Therefore, immediately preceding the regular run, the teacher was given a preliminary series of ten words to read to the learner. There were three neutral words in the practice series (i.e., words that the learner answered correctly), so that shocks were administered for seven of the words, with the maximum shock at 105 volts (moderate shock). Almost all subjects mastered the procedure by the time the preliminary run was over.

    Subjects are then presented with a second list, and are told that the procedure is the same as for the first list; the experimenter adds, however:

    'When you get to the bottom of the list, repeat it over again, and continue giving shocks, until the learner has learned all the pairs correctly.'

    The experimenter instructs the subject to:

    'Start from 15 volts and increase the shock level one step each time the learner gives a wrong answer.'

2. No subject who reached the 30th shock level ever refused to continue using it.

3. David Mark Mantell, 'The Potential for Violence in Germany', *Journal of Social Issues*, Vol. 27, No. 4 (November 4, 1971), pp. 101-12.

4. Within the last decade the effects of physical proximity on behaviour have come under critical examination. See, for example, Edward T. Hall, *The Hidden Dimension* (New York: Doubleday, 1966).

5. Recently, I have learned that other experimenters (Sheridan and King, 1972) have replicated the obedience experiments but with this difference: in place of a human victim, they used a genuine

victim, a puppy, who actually received the electric shock and who yelped, howled, and ran when he was shocked. Men and women were used as subjects, and the authors found that the women were more compliant than the men. Indeed, they write: 'Without exception, female S's complied with instructions to shock the puppy all the way to the end of the scale.' See also Kilham and Mann, 1972.

6. This is borne out by examining the data on reported nervousness. At the conclusion of his performance, each subject indicated on a scale just how tense or nervous he was at the point of maximum tension. These data are available for twenty-one experimental conditions, including the present one, and obedient women report higher tension than any of the twenty groups of obedient males. This may be due to the fact that the women were more nervous than the men, or simply that they felt freer to report it. In any case, for those women who were obedient, the reported tension exceeded that of any of the twenty other conditions. However, this is not true of the defiant women. Their reports of nervousness fall out just about in the middle of the distribution for male defiant subjects.

7. See study by Hofling et al. on the failure of nurses to question doctors' orders on drug overdoses. Charles K. Hofling, E. Brotzman, S. Dalrymple, N. Graves, C. Pierce, 'An Experimental Study in Nurse-Physician Relationships', *The Journal of Nervous and Mental Disease*, Vol. 143, No. 2 (1966), pp. 171-80.

8. The assertion that the content of the command may itself be largely responsible for the effects is not gratuitous. Numerous studies in social psychology demonstrate the effects that peers, lacking any particular authority, may exercise on an individual (Asch, 1951; Milgram, 1964).

9. Conformity is, as de Tocqueville shrewdly observed, the logical regulatory mechanism of democratised relations among men. It is 'democratic' in the sense that the pressure it places on the target is not to make him better or worse than those exerting the pressure but merely to make him the same.

    Obedience arises out of and perpetuates inequalities in human relationships and thus, in its ultimate expression, is the ideal regulatory mechanism of fascism. It is only logical that a philosophy of government that has human inequality as its touchstone will also elevate obedience as an absolute virtue. Obedient behaviour is initiated in the context of a hierarchical social structure and has as its outcome the differentiation of behaviour between superior and subordinate. It is no accident that the hallmark of the Third Reich was its emphasis both on the concept of superior and inferior groups and on quick, impressive, and prideful obedience, with clicking boots and the ready execution of command.

10. I have oversimplified. While it is true that nature is rich in hierarchical organisations, it is not the case that men need function within them at all times. An isolated brain cell cannot survive apart from its larger organ system. But an individual's relative self-sufficiency frees him from total dependence on larger social systems. He has the capacity both to merge into such systems, through the assumption of roles, or to separate himself from them. This capacity for dual functioning confers on the species maximum adaptive advantages. It assures the power, security, and efficiency that derives from organisation, along with the innovative potential and flexible response of the individual. From the standpoint of species survival it is the best of both worlds.

11. Students of child development have long recognised that 'the first social relationship is one of recognising and complying with the suggestions of authority' (English, 1961, page 24). The initial conditions of total dependency give the child little choice in the matter. And authority generally presents itself to the infant in a benign and helpful form. Nonetheless, it has been commonly observed that at the age of two or three the infant enters a period of unrestrained negativism in which he challenges authority at virtually every turn, rejecting even its most benign demands. Stogdill (1936) reports that of all behaviour problems of social adjustment, parents rank disobedience as the most serious. Frequently there is intense conflict between child and parent at this point, and maturational processes, abetted by parental insistence, ordinarily bring the child to a more compliant disposition. *The child's interminable disobedience, however much it constitutes a rejection of authority and assertion of self, differs from adult*

disobedience in that it takes place without any conception of individual responsibility on the child's part. Unlike the forms of disobedience we may come to value in the adult, it is an indiscriminate, purely expressive form of defiance that is not grounded in moral concerns.

12. The technical problem of how authority communicates its legitimacy is worth serious thought. Consider that when a young man receives a letter that claims to be from his draft board, what evidence is there that the entire operation is not simply an extended prank? And if we are to carry this further, what is the evidence that when the boy appears at a camp designated by the board, the men in khaki really have the right to take charge of his life? Perhaps it is all a gigantic hoax perpetrated by a contingent of unemployed actors. Genuine authority, because it recognises the ease with which the appearance of authority may be fabricated, must be extremely vigilant of counterfeit authority, and the penalties for falsely claiming authority are severe.

13. Imagine an experimenter travelling from one house to the next in a private residential district and, with permission, setting up his experiments in the living rooms of those homes. His aura of authority would be weaker without the laboratory setting that ordinarily buttresses his position.

14. For the concept of 'zone of indifference', see Herbert A. Simon, *Administrative Behaviour: A Study of Decision-Making Processes in Administrative Organisations.* New York: The Free Press, 1965.

15. *The Caine Mutiny*, by Herman Wouk (1952), illustrates this situation well. It is all right for an authority to be stupid. Many persons of authority function exceedingly well even if they are incompetent. The problem arises only when an authority, taking advantage of his position, forces his more competent subordinates to follow a wrong course of action. Stupid authorities can sometimes he very effective and even be loved by their subordinates, as long as they assign responsibility to the talented subordinates. *The Caine Mutiny* illustrates two additional points. First, how difficult it is to defy authority even when authority is incompetent. Only after great inner stress and turmoil did Willie and Keith take over the Caine, though it was on its way to being sunk because of Queeg's incompetence. Second, despite what

appeared to be virtually absolute requirement that the mutiny occur, the attachment to principles of authority was so profound, that the author, through the voice of Greenwald, in a dramatic turn of events, called into question the moral basis of the mutiny.

16. In *Group Psychology and Analysis of the Ego* (1921), Freud pointed out that a person suppresses his own superego functions, allowing the leader full right to decide what is good or bad.

17. Koestler notes in his brilliant analysis of social hierarchies: 'I have repeatedly stressed that the selfish impulses of man constitute a much lesser historic danger than his integrative tendencies. To put it in the simplest way: the individual who indulges in an excess of aggressive self-assertiveness incurs the penalties of society – he outlaws himself, he contracts out of the hierarchy. The true believer, on the other hand, becomes more closely knit into it; he enters the womb of his church, or party, or whatever the social holon to which he surrenders his identity.' Arthur Koestler, *The Ghost in the Machine* (New York: The Macmillan Company, 1967), Part III, 'Disorder', p. 246.

18. An interpretation consistent with the theory of cognitive dissonance. See L. Festinger, 1957.

19. See Erving Goffman, 'Embarrassment and Social Organisation', *The American Journal of Sociology*, Vol. 62 (November 1956), pp. 264–71. See also Andre Modigliani, 'Embarrassment and Embarrassability', *Sociometry*, Vol. 31, No. 3 (September 1968), pp. 313–26; and 'Embarrassment Facework, and Eye Contact: Testing a Theory of Embarrassment', *Journal of Personality and Social Psychology*, Vol. 17, No. 1 (1971), pp. 15–24.

20. If embarrassment and shame are important forces holding the subject to his obedient role, we ought to find a sharp drop in obedience when the preconditions for the experience of these emotions are eliminated. This is precisely what occurred in Experiment 7, when the experimenter departed from the laboratory and gave his orders by telephone. Much of the obedience shown by our subjects was rooted in the face-to-face nature of the social occasion. Some types of obedience – say, that of a soldier sent on a solitary mission behind enemy lines – require extended exposure to the authority in question and a congruence between the values of the subordinate and his

authority.

Both the studies of Garfinkel and the present experiment indicated that the assumptive structure of social life needed to be disrupted if disobedience was to occur. The same awkwardness, embarrassment, and difficulty in being disobedient occurs as in Garfinkel's (1964) demonstrations, in which people are asked to violate suppositions of everyday life.

21. It is the failure to grasp the transformation into a state of agency and an inadequate understanding of the forces that bind the person into it that account for the almost total inability to predict the behaviour in question. Those judging the situation think it is the ordinary person, with his full moral capacities operating, when they predict his breakoff from the experiment. They do not take into account in the least the fundamental reorganisation of a person's mental life that occurs by virtue of entry into an authority system.

The quickest way to correct the erroneous prediction of persons who do not know the outcome of the experiment is to say to them, 'The content of the action is not half so important as you think; the relationship among the actors is twice as important. Base your prediction not on what the participants say or do, but on how they relate to each other in terms of a social structure.'

There is a further reason why people do not correctly predict the behaviour. Society promotes the ideology that an individual's actions stem from his character. This ideology has the pragmatic effect of stimulating people to act *as if* they alone controlled their behaviour. This is, however, a seriously distorted view of the determinants of human action, and does not allow for accurate prediction.

22. Konrad Lorenz describes the disturbance in inhibitory mechanisms brought about by the interposition of tools and weapons: 'The same principle applies, to even a greater degree, to the use of modern remote control weapons. The man who presses the releasing button is so completely screened against seeing, hearing, or otherwise emotionally realising the consequences of his action that he can commit it with impunity – even if he is burdened with the power of imagination.' Konrad Lorenz, *On Aggression* (New York: Harcourt Brace Jovanovich, 1966), p. 234.

23. See N. J. Lerner, 'Observer's Evaluation of a Victim: Justice, Guilt, and Veridical Perception', *Journal of Personality and Social Psychology*, Vol. 20, No. 2 (1971), pp. 127-35.

24. In Princeton: D. Rosenhan, 'Obedience and Rebellion: Observations on the Milgram Three-Party Paradigm'.

   In Munich: D. M. Mantell, 'The Potential for Violence in Germany'. *Journal of Social Issues*, Vol. 27, No. 4 (1971), pp. 101-12.

   In Rome: Leonardo Ancona and Rosetta Parevson, 'Contributo allo studie della aggressione: La Dinamica della obbedienza distruttiva', *Archiva di psicologia neurologia e psichiatria*, Anna XXIX (1968), fasc. IV.

   In Australia: W. Kilham and L. Mann, 'Level of Destructive Obedience as a Function of Transmittor and Executant Roles in the Milgram Obedience Paradigm'. (1973) *Journal of Personality and Social Psychology*.

25. See M. I. Orne and C. C. Holland, for example, and my response to them in: A. G. Miller (ed.) *The Social Psychology of Psychological Research*. New York: The Free Press, 1972.

26. But we must not be naïve on this point. We have all seen how government, with its control of the propaganda apparatus invariably portrays its goals in morally favourable terms; how, in our own country, the destruction of men, women, and children in Vietnam was justified by reference to saving the Free World, etc. We see, also, how easily the pronouncements are accepted as legitimising goals. Dictatorships attempt to persuade the masses by justifying their programs in terms of established values. Even Hitler did not say that he would destroy the Jews because of hatred but because of his wish to purify the Aryan race and create a higher civilisation free of enfeebling vermin.

27. Bierstedt points out quite correctly that the phenomenon of authority is more fundamental even than that of government: '. . .The problem of authority rests at the very bottom of an adequate theory of the social structure . . . even government, in a sense, is not merely a political phenomenon but primarily and fundamentally a social phenomenon, and . . . the matrix from which government springs itself possesses an order and a structure. If anarchy is the contrary of government, so anomy is the contrary of society. Authority, in other words, is by no means

a purely political phenomenon in the narrow sense of the word. For it is not only in the political organisation of society, but in all of its organisation, that authority appears. Each association in society, no matter how small or how temporary it might be, has its own structure of authority' Bierstedt, pp. 68-69.

28. But the plea of 'superior orders' was made by Lieutenant William Calley, who commanded the platoon that carried out the action. The military prosecutor challenged Calley's plea of superior orders. Instructively, the prosecutor did not contest the principle that a soldier must obey orders, but charged that Calley acted without orders, and therefore, was responsible for the massacre. Calley was adjudged guilty.

The reaction of the American public to the Calley trial was studied by Kelman and Lawrence (1972), and their findings are not reassuring. Fifty-one percent of the sample indicated that they would follow orders if commanded to shoot all inhabitants of a Vietnamese village. Kelman concludes:

'Clearly, not everyone finds the demands of apparently legitimate authorities equally compelling. Not all of Milgram's subjects shocked their victims with the highest voltage. Nor did every soldier under Calley's command follow his orders to kill unarmed civilians. Those who resist in such circumstances have apparently managed to retain the framework of personal causation and responsibility that we ordinarily use in daily life.

'Yet, our data suggest that many Americans feel they have no right to resist authoritative demands. They regard Calley's actions at My Lai as normal, even desirable, because (they think) he performed them in obedience to legitimate authority.'

We need to ask why Kelman's respondents see themselves as complying with military authority at My Lai (when few – if any – would have predicted submission to the experimenter's authority).

First, the interview response, secured while the country was at war in Vietnam, reflected attitudes toward the war itself and indicated general support for the government's policies. If the questions had been asked in peacetime, a larger proportion would have predicted disobedience. The response also expressed solidarity with an American soldier who most Americans felt should not have been brought to trial. Second, raising the question of obedience in a military context places it in the setting that is most familiar to the average person: he knows that a soldier is supposed to obey orders, and his interview response springs from folk wisdom, hearsay, and knowledge of the military context. Yet this does not presume any understanding of general principles of obedience, which can only be demonstrated by their correct application to a novel context. People understand that soldiers massacre, but they fail to see that an action such as this, routinely carried out, is the logical outcome of processes that are at work in less visible form through out organised society. Finally, the response indicates the degree to which the American people had embraced the viewpoint of authority in evaluating the Vietnam War. They had been thoroughly indoctrinated by government propaganda (which, at the societal level is the means whereby an official definition of the situation is promulgated). In this sense, the respondents to Kelman's question did not reside completely outside the authority system they were asked to comment upon but had already been influenced by it.

29. Henry Wirz, *Trial of Henry Wirz* (Commandant at Andersonville), House of Representatives, 40th Congress, 2d Session, Ed. Doc. No. 23. (Letter from the Secretary of War Ad Interim, in answer to a resolution of the House of April 16, 1866, transmitting a summary of the trial of Henry Wirz. Dec. 17, 1867.

30. It would seem that the anarchist argument for universal dismantling of political institutions is a powerful solution to the problem of authority. But the problems of anarchism are equally insoluble. First, while the existence of authority sometimes leads to the commission of ruthless and immoral acts, the absence of authority renders one a victim to such acts on the part of others who are better organised. Were the United States to abandon all forms of political authority, the outcome would be entirely clear. We would soon become the victims of our own disorganisation, because better organised societies would immediately perceive and act on the opportunities that weakness creates.

Moreover, it would be an oversimplification to present the picture of the noble individual in a continuous struggle against malevolent authority. The obvious truth is that much of his nobility, the very values he brings to bear against malevolent authority, are themselves derived from authority. And for every individual who carries out harsh action because of authority, there is another individual who is restrained from doing so.

31. See Jay Katz, *Experimentation with Human Beings: The Authority of the Investigator, Subject, Professions, and State in the Human Experimentation Process*, New York: Russell Sage Foundation, (1972). This source book of 1159 pages contains commentaries on the present experiments by Baumrind, Elms, Kelman, Ring, and Milgram. It also includes the statement of Dr Paul Errera, who interviewed a number of participants in the experiment (page 400). Thoughtful discussions of the ethical issues of this research can be found in A. Miller, *The Social Psychology of Psychological Research*, and in A. Elms, *Social Psychology and Social Relevance*.

REFERENCES

Abse, D. *The Dogs of Pavlov*. London: Valentine, Mitchell & Co., Ltd.

Adorno, T.; Frenkel-Brunswik, Else; Levinson, D. J., and Sanford, R. N. *The Authoritarian Personality*. New York: Harper & Row, 1950.

Arendt, H. *Eichmann in Jerusalem: A Report on the Banality of Evil*. New York: Viking Press, 1963.

Asch, J. E. 'Effects of Group Pressure upon the Modification and Distortion of Judgement'. In H. Guetzkow (ed.), *Groups, Leadership, and Men*. Pittsburgh: Carnegie Press, 1951.

Ashby, W. R. *An Introduction to Cybernetics*. London: Chapman and Hall Ltd., 1956

Baumrind, D 'Some Thoughts on Ethics of Research: After Reading Milgram's "Behavioural Study of Obedience."' *American Psychologist*, Vol. 19 (1964), pp. 421-23.

Berkowitz, L. Aggression: *A Social Psychological Analysis*. New York: McGraw-Hill, 1962.

Bettelheim, B. *The Informed Heart*. New York: The Free Press, 1960.

Bierstedt, R. 'The Problem of Authority'. Chapter 3 in *Freedom and Control in Modern Society*. New York: Van Nostrand, 1954, pp. 67-81.

Block, J. and J. 'An Interpersonal Experiment on Reactions to Authority'. *Human Relations*, Vol. 5 (1952), pp. 91-98.

Buss, A. H. *The Psychology of Aggression*. New York: John Wiley, 1961

Cannon, W. B. *The Wisdom of the Body*. New York: W. W. Norton, 1932

Cartwright, D. (ed.). *Studies in Social Power*. Ann Arbor: University of Michigan Press, 1959.

Comfort, A. *Authority and Delinquency in the Modern State: A Criminological Approach to the Problem of Power*. London: Routledge and K. Paul, 1950.

Crawford, T. 'In Defense of Obedience Research: An Extension of the Kelman Ethic', In A.G. Miller (ed.), *The Social Psychology of Psychological Research*. New York: The Free Press, 1972, pp. 197-86.

Dicks, H.V. *Licensed Mass Murder: A Socio-Psychological Study of Some*

S.S. Killers. New York: Basic Books, 1972.

Elms, A. C. 'Acts of Submission'. Chapter 4 of *Social Psychology and Social Relevance.* Boston: Little, Brown, 1972.

English, H. B. *Dynamics of Child Development.* New York: Holt, Rinehart and Winston, 1961.

Erikson, M. 'The Inhumanity of Ordinary People'. *International Journal of Psychiatry,* Vol. 6 (1968), pp. 278-79.

Etzioni, A. 'A Model of Significant Research'. *International Journal of Psychiatry,* Vol 6 (1968), pp 279-80.

Feinberg, I. 'Sex Differences in Resistance to Group Pressure'. Unpublished master's thesis, Swarthmore College, Swarthmore, Pa.

Festinger, L. *A Theory of Cognitive Dissonance.* New York: Harper & Row, 1957.

Frank, J. D. 'Experimental Studies of Personal Pressure and Resistance'. *Journal of Genetic Psychology,* Vol. 30 (1944), pp. 23-64

French, J. R. P. 'A Formal Theory of Social Power'. *Psychological Review,* Vol. 63 (1956), pp. 181-94

– ; Morrison, H. W., and Levinger, G. 'Coercive Power and Forces Affecting Conformity'. *Journal of Abnormal Social Psychology,* Vol. 61 (1960), pp. 93-101.

– , and Raven, B. H. 'The Bases of Social Power'. In D. Cartwright (ed.), *Studies in Social Power.* Ann Arbor: University of Michigan Press, 1959, pp. 150-67.

Freud, S. *Totem and Taboo.* Translated by J. Strachey. New York: W. W. Norton, 1950.

– . 'Thoughts for the Times on War and Death'. In J. Strachey (ed.), *The Standard Edition of the Complete Psychological Works of Sigmund Freud,* Vol. 14. London: The Hogarth Press, 1957, pp. 273-302.

– . *Group Psychology and the Analysis of the Ego.* Translated by J. Strachey. London: Hogarth, 1922; New York: Bantam Books, 1960. (German original, 1921.)

Fromm, E. *Escape from Freedom.* New York: Holt, Rinehart and Winston, 1941.

Garfinkel, H. 'Studies of the Routine Grounds of Everyday Activities'. *Social Problems,* Vol 11 (Winter 1964), pp. 225-50.

Glasser, R. J. *365 Days.* New York: George Braziller 1971.

Goffman, E. *The Presentation of Self in Everyday Life.* New York: Doubleday Anchor Books, 1959

– . 'Embarrassment and Social Organization'. *The American Journal of Sociology*, Vol. 62 (November 1956), pp 264-71.

Halberstam, David. *Making of a Quagmire*. New York: Random House, 1965

Hall, E. T. *The Hidden Dimension*. New York: Doubleday, 1966.

Hillberg, R. *The Destruction of the European Jews*. Chicago: Quadrangle Books, 1961.

Hobbes, Thomas. *Leviathan*. Oxford: Oxford University Press, 1909. Reproduction of 1651 edition.

Hoffing, C. K.; Brotzman, E.; Dalrymple, S.; Graves, N., and Pierce, C. 'An Experimental Study of Nurse-Physician Relations'. *The Journal of Nervous and Mental Disease*. Vol. 143, No. 2 (1966), pp. 171-80.

Homans, G. C. Social Behavior: *Its Elementary Forms*. New York: Harcourt Brace Jovanovich, 1961.

Katz, J. *Experimentation with Human Beings: The Authority of the Investigator, Subject, Professions, and State in the Human Experimentation Process*. New York: Russell Sage Foundation, 1972.

Kelman, H. 'Human Use of Human Subjects: The Problem of Deception in Social Psychological Experiments'. *Psychological Bulletin*, Vol. 67 (1967), pp. 1-11.

– , and Lawrence, L. 'Assignment of Responsibility in the Case of Lt. Calley: Preliminary Report on a National Survey'. *Journal of Social Issues*, Vol. 28, No. 1 (1972).

Kierkegaard, S. *Fear and Trembling*. English edition. Princeton: Princeton University Press, 1941.

Kilham, W., and Mann, L. 'Level of Destructive Obedience as a Function of Transmittor and Executant Roles in the Milgram Obedience Paradigm'. *Journal of Personality and Social Psychology*.

Koestler, Arthur. *The Ghost in the Machine*. New York: Macmillan, 1967.

Kohlberg, L. 'Development of Moral Character and Moral Ideology'. In Hoffman, M. L., and Hoffman, L. W. (eds.), *Review of Child Development Research*, Vol. 1. New York: Russell Sage Foundation, 1964, pp. 383-431.

– . 'Relationships Between the Development of Moral Judgment and Moral Conduct'. Paper presented at Symposium on Behavioural and Cognitive Concepts in the Study of Internationalization at the Society for Research in Child Development, Minneapolis,

Minnesota, March 26, 1956.

Laski, H. J. 'The Dangers of Obedience'. *Harper's Monthly Magazine*, Vol. 159 (1919), pp. 1-10.

Lazarus, R. 'A Laboratory Approach to the Dynamics of Psychological Stress'. *American Psychologist*, Vol. 19 (1964), pp. 400-411.

Leavitt, S. 'The Andersonville Trial'. In Bennett Cerf (ed.), *Four Contemporary American Plays*. New York: Random House, 1961.

Lerner, M. J. 'Observer's Evaluation of a Victim: Justice, Guilt, and Veridical Perception'. *Journal of Personality and Social Psychology*, Vol. 20, No. 2 (1971), pp. 127-35.

Lewin, K. *Field Theory in Social Science*. New York: Harper & Row, 1951.

Lippett, R. 'Field Theory and Experiment in Social Psychology: Autocratic and Democratic Group Atmosphere'. *American Journal of Sociology*, Vol. 45, pp. 25-49.

Lorenz, K. *On Aggression*. Translated by M. K. Wilson. New York: Bantam Books, 1963.

Mantell, D. M. 'The Potential for Violence in Germany'. *Journal of Social Issues*, Vol. 27, No. 4 (1971), pp. 101-12.

Marler, P. *Mechanisms of Animal Behavior*. New York: John Wiley & Sons, 1967.

Milgram, S. 'Behavioural Study of Obedience'. *Journal of Abnormal Psychology*, Vol. 67 (1963), pp. 371-78.

– . 'Dynamics of Obedience: Experiments in Social Psychology'. Mimeographed report, National Science Foundation, Jan. 25, 1961.

– . 'Group Pressure and Action Against a Person'. *Journal of Abnormal Social Psychology*, Vol. 69 (1964), pp. 137-43.

– . 'Issues in the Study of Obedience: A Reply to Baumrind'. *American Psychologist*, Vol. 19 (1964), pp. 848-52.

– . 'Liberating Effects of Group Pressure'. *Journal of Personality and Social Psychology*, Vol. 1 (1965), pp. 127-34.

– . *Obedience* (a filmed experiment). Distributed by the New York University Film Library. Copyright 1965.

– . 'Some Conditions of Obedience and Disobedience to Authority'. *Human Relations*, Vol. 18, No. 1 (1965), pp. 57-76

– . 'Interpreting Obedience: Error and Evidence; A Reply to Orne and Holland'. In A. G. Miller (ed.), *The Social Psychology of Psychological Research*. New York: The Free Press, 1972.

Miller, A. (ed.). *The Social Psychology of Psychological Research*. New York: The Free Press, 1972.

Miller, N. 'Experimental Studies of Conflict'. In M. J. Hunt (ed.), *Personality and Behavior Disorders*. New York: Ronald Press, 1944, pp. 431-65.

Modigliani, A. 'Embarrassment and Embarrassability'. *Sociometry*, Vol. 31, No. 3 (September 1968), pp. 313-26.

– . 'Embarrassment, Facework, and Eye Contact: Testing a Theory of Embarrassment'. *Journal of Personality and Social Psychology*. Vol. 17, No.1 (1971), pp. 15-24.

Orne, M. T., and Holland, C. C. 'On the Ecological Validity of Laboratory Deceptions'. *International Journal of Psychiatry*, Vol. 6, No. 4 (1968), pp. 282-93.

Orwell, G. *Selected Essays*. London: Penguin Books, 1957.

Raven, B. H. 'Social Influence and Power'. In I. D. Steiner and M. Fishbein (eds.), *Current Studies in Social Psychology*. New York: Holt, Rinehart and Winston, 1965.

– , and French, J. R. P. 'Group Support, Legitimate Power, and Social Influence'. *Journal of Personality*, Vol. 26 (1958), pp. 400-409.

Rescher, N. *The Logic of Commands*. New York: Dover Publications, 1966.

Rosenhan, D. 'Some Origins of Concerns for Others'. In P. H. Mussen, J. Langer, and M. Covington (eds.), *Trends and Issues in Developmental Psychology*. New York: Holt, Rinehart and Winston, 1969, pp. 134-53.

– . *Obedience and Rebellion: Observations on the Milgram Three-Party Paradigm*.

Rosenthal, R., and Rosnow, R. L. 'Volunteer Subjects and the Results of Opinion Change Studies'. *Psychological Reports*, Vol. 19 (1966), p.1183.

Scott, J. P. *Aggression*. Chicago: University of Chicago Press, 1958.

Sheridan, C. L., and King, R. G. 'Obedience to Authority with an Authentic Victim'. Proceedings, Eightieth Annual Convention, *American Psychological Association*. 1972, pp. 165-66.

Sherif, M. *The Psychology of Social Norms*. New York: Harper & Row, 1936.

Shirer, W. L. *The Rise and Fall of the Third Reich*. New York: Simon & Schuster, 1960.

Sidis, B. *The Psychology of Suggestion*, New York: Appleton, 1898

Simon, H. A. *Administrative Behavior: A Study of Decision-Making Processes in Administrative Organizations*. New York: The Free Press, 1965.

Snow, C. P. 'Either-Or'. *Progressive*, February 1961, p. 24.

Sophocles. *Antigone*. Translated by J. J. Chapmam. Boston: Houghton Mifflin Co., 1930

Stogdill, R. M. 'The Measurement of Attitudes Toward Parental Control and the Social Adjustment of Children'. *Journal of Applied Psychology*, Vol. 20 (1936), 259-61.

Taylor, T. *Nuremberg and Vietnam: An American Tragedy*. Chicago: Quadrangle Books, 1970.

Tinbergen, N. *Social Behavior in Animals*. London: Butler and Tanner, Ltd., 1953

Thoreau, Henry David. *Walden and Civil Disobedience*. Edited by Sherman Paul. Boston: Houghton Mifflin, 1957.

Tocqueville, Alexis de. *Democracy in America*. London: Oxford University Press, 1965.

Tolstoy, L. *Tolstoy's Writings on Civil Disobedience and Non-violence*. New York: New American Library, 1968.

Weber, M. *Theory of Social and Economic Organization*. Oxford: Oxford University Press, 1947.

Wouk, H. *The Caine Mutiny*. Garden City: Doubleday and Company, 1952.

Other Works Consulted

Adams, J. Stacy, and Romney, A. Kimball. 'A Functional Analysis of Authority'. *Psychological Review*, Vol. 66, No. 4 (July 1959), pp. 234-51.

Aronfreed, Justin. *Conduct and Conscience: The Socialization of Internalized Control over Behavior*. New York: Academic Press, 1968.

Berkowitz, Leonard, and Lundy, R. 'Personality Characteristics Related to Susceptibility to Influence by Peers or Authority Figures'. *Journal of Personality*, Vol. 25 (1957), pp. 306-16.

Binet, A. *La Suggestibilité*. Paris: Schleicher, 1900.

Cohn, Norman. *Warrant for Genocide*. New York: Harper & Row, 1967.

DeGrazia, Sebastian. 'What Authority Is Not'. *The American Political*

Science Review, Vol. 3 (June 1959).

Eatherly, Claude. Burning Conscience: *The Case of the Hiroshima Pilot Told in His Letters to Gunther Anders.* New York: Monthly Review Press, 1961.

Elkins, Stanley M. *Slavery: A Problem in American Institutional and Intellectual Life.* Chicago: The University of Chicago Press, 1959.

Friedlander, Saul. *Kurt Gerstein: The Ambiguity of Good.* New York: Alfred A. Knopf, 1969.

Friedrich, C. J. *Authority.* Cambridge: Harvard University Press, 1958.

Camson, William. *Power and Discontent.* Homewood, Ill.: The Dorsey Press, 1968.

Gaylin, W. *In the Service of Their Country: War Resisters in Prison.* New York: The Viking Press, 1970.

Goldhammer, H., and Shils, E. 'Types of Power and Status'. *American Journal of Sociology,* Vol. 45 (1939), pp. 171–78.

Gurr, Ted Robert. *Why Men Rebel.* Princeton: Princeton University Press, 1970

Hallie, Philip P. *The Paradox of Cruelty.* Middletown, Conn.: Wesleyan University Press, 1969.

Hammer, Richard. *The Court Martial of Lt. Calley.* New York: Coward McCann, & Geoghegan, 1971.

Heydecker, J. J., and Leeb, J. *The Nuremberg Trial.* Cleveland and New York: World Publishing Company, 1962

Howton, F. William. *Functionaries.* Chicago: Quadrangle Books, 1969.

Huntington, Samuel P. *The Soldier and the State: The Theory and Politics of Civil-Military Relations.* New York: Vintage Books, 1964.

Lasswell, H. D., and Kaplan, A. *Power and Society.* New Haven, Conn..: Yale University Press, 1950.

Lauman, Edward O.; Siegel, Paul M., and Hodge, Robert W. (eds.). *The Logic of Social Hierarchies.* Chicago: Markham Publishing Co., 1970.

Neuman, Franz. *The Democratic and the Authoritarian State: Essays in Political and Legal Theory.* Edited by Herbert Marcuse. New York: The Free Press, 1957.

Parsons, T. *The Social System.* New York: The Free Press, 1951.

Reich, Wilhelm. *The Mass Psychology of Fascism.* New York: Orgone Institute Press, 1946.

Ring, K.; Wallston, K., and Corey, M. 'Mode of Debriefing as a Factor Affecting Subjective Reaction to a Milgram-Type Obedience

Experiment: An Ethical Inquiry'. *Representative Research in Social Psychology*, Vol. 1 (1970), pp. 67-88.

Rokeach, M. 'Authority, Authoritarianism, and Conformity'. In I. A. Berg and B. M. Bass (eds.), *Conformity and Deviation*. New York: Harper & Row, 1961, pp. 230-57.

Russell, Bertrand. *Authority and the Individual*. Boston: Beacon Press, 1949.

Sack, John. *Lt. Calley: His Own Story*. New York: The Viking Press, 1970.

Speer, Albert. *Inside the Third Reich: Memoirs*. New York: Macmillan, 1970

Tilker, H. A. 'Socially Responsible Behavior as a Function of Observer Responsibility and Victim Feedback'. *Journal of Personality and Social Psychology*, Vol. 14, No. 2 (February 1970), pp. 95-100.

Von Mises, Ludwig. *Bureaucracy*. New Haven, Conn.: Yale University Press, 1944.

Whyte, L. L., Wilson, A. G., and Wilson, D. (eds.). *Hierarchical Structures*. New York: American Elsevier Publishing, 1969.

Wolfe, D. M. 'Power and Authority in the Family'. In D. Cartwright (ed.) *Studies in Social Power*. Ann Arbor: University of Michigan Press, 1959, pp. 99-117.

INDEX

also from **Pinter & Martin** *by* **Stanley Milgram**

The Individual in a Social World

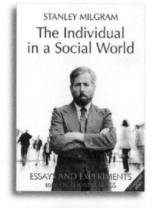

Stanley Milgram revolutionized our understanding of human nature with his classic research on obedience to authority – but the obedience experiments form just a small part of an extraordinary wealth of ground-breaking research that made him one of the most important social psychologists of our times.

By the time the first edition of *The Individual in a Social World* appeared in 1977, Milgram had moved beyond obedience to other innovative research, such as the psychology of city life, the small world phenomenon (also known as 'six degrees of separation'), mental maps of cities, the lost-letter technique, the familiar stranger, as well as a large-scale experiment on media influence, which is still unique to the present day. In 1992, a second, posthumous edition appeared containing additional articles which Milgram had written after the first edition.

This third, expanded edition of *The Individual in a Social World* combines articles that appeared in both of the earlier editions as well as previously uncollected material. Among the latter is, for example, an article in which Milgram provides a perspective on the Jonestown massacre and then uses it as a stepping stone for a ringing affirmation of the power of situational determinants of behavior. Another article, 'The Social Meaning of Fanaticism,' is almost uncanny in its relevance to our times, despite the fact that it was written several decades ago, as is his take on the potential impact of the Internet in 'Network Love'.

Stanley Milgram possessed a relentless curiosity about the hidden workings of our social world, which he tried to make visible through his experiments and think pieces brought together in this unique, revealing and engaging book – a must-read for anyone interested in social psychology.

paperback | ISBN 978-1-905177-12-7 | RRP £19.95

visit **www.pinterandmartin.com**
for further information, extracts and special offers